WORLD WAR I
IN PHOTOGRAPHS

WORLD WAR I
IN PHOTOGRAPHS

ADRIAN GILBERT
CONSULTANT EDITOR JOHN TERRAINE

BLACK CAT

Editor Richard Williams
Designer Michael Moule

Photograph, previous page: Australian bayonet-charge at
Gallipoli, December 1915.
Photograph, half-title page: British infantryman returning from
the front, 1918.
Photograph, endpapers: German infantry assault on the
Western Front.

Photographs were supplied by the Australian War Memorial,
Bundesarchiv, Bayerisches Hauptstaatsarchiv, ECPA, Robert
Hunt Library, Imperial War Museum, Musée de la Guerre,
Obrazové Zprovodajstvíčtk, US War Department General Staff,
US Signal Corps, and VHÚ Prague.

The author would like to thank the librarian and staff of the Royal
United Services Institute, the Department of Photographs at the
Imperial War Museum, the Robert Hunt Library, and, most
especially, Sally Payne.

The Department of Photographs at the Imperial War Museum,
London, has a visitors' room where the Museum's extensive
collection of World War I and World War II material may be
studied, and where copies of many of the photographs
reproduced in this book are available for purchase.

First published in Great Britain 1986 by Orbis
Book Publishing Corporation
Reprinted 1988 by Macdonald & Co (Publishers) Ltd
under the Black Cat imprint

Macdonald & Co (Publishers) Ltd
3rd Floor, Greater London House,
Hampstead Road, London NW1 7QX

a member of Maxwell Pergamon Publishing Corporation plc

ISBN 0-7481-0148-9

Printed in Great Britain by
Purnell Book Production Limited
Member of the BPCC Group

Contents

Introduction

To seek a single cause for an event so massive and far-reaching as World War I is clearly ridiculous. It can only be attributed to a multiplicity of factors; an even simpler conclusion was expressed by the American Ambassador in London in August 1914: 'It *had* to come.'

Within that inevitability of conflict, and within the multiplicity of motives for it, however, the Ambassador singled out German militarism as a main trigger of war in 1914. It was natural for the Allied powers, at the time, to blame Germany for starting the war; it was natural that when the Peace Treaty was signed in 1919 it should contain a 'war-guilt' clause which planted this blame squarely upon the Germans; and it was natural that the Germans themselves should resent this very much. Those who looked for *rapprochement* between all countries between the wars rejected the concept of German guilt because it was a source of bitterness and thus a threat to peace. Nazi propagan-

Far right: Emperor Franz Joseph, monarch of the multi-national Austro-Hungarian Empire.

Right, below: The man who lit the first spark, Gavrilo Princip – the assassin of the emperor's heir, Archduke Franz Ferdinand.

Below: Kaiser Wilhelm II with the King of Italy, shortly before the outbreak of war.

Above: Archduke Franz Ferdinand and his wife set off on their fateful ride through Sarajevo, 28 June 1914.

Below: Austrian troops are mobilised for war. A dispute between Serbia and Austria-Hungary was to develop into world war in a matter of weeks.

da exploited these feelings to present Germany as a wronged nation, no more 'guilty' than any other. In the 1960s and 1970s, however, a new school of German historians re-examined the subject and basically returned to the belief that German militarism *was* to blame after all. And this has largely been accepted by a younger British school, subscribing to the dictum of Dr Paul Kennedy in 1979: '. . . it was only the German plan which involved an attack upon another power (France), whether or not the latter wished to become involved in the war; it was only the German plan which involved the violation of neutral territory simply to satisfy military exigencies; and most important of all – it was only in the German plan that mobilisation meant war.'

It thus becomes clear that Germany – German policy, and the instrument on which it depended, the German Army – stands at the centre of the action. It is not possible to comprehend World War I otherwise; from August 1914 until August 1918, all the fundamental initiatives of the war were German, and their enemies were in effect dancing to the German tune. This explains much that is otherwise unintelligible: the predominance of the Western Front, the necessity for the costly offensives which took place there, the ineffectiveness of traditional British maritime strategy (it had never been tried against powers existing in the *centre* of Europe), and much else besides.

If Germany provided the mainspring of action, it was the world system of alliances that dictated the shape of the war, above all the fact that it would be a *world* war. The alliances have been much blamed, as evidence of warlike intention, but the truth is that their purpose was not war but peace: they were an investment in security – an investment which then seemed sensible, but as we know proved to be founded on vain hope. Thus what began as a quarrel between Austria and Serbia arising from the murder of the heir to the Austrian throne in June 1914 immediately drew in Russia in support of Serbia, and Germany in support of Austria (by the terms of the central alliance). Russian involvement was the signal for Germany's immediate attack on Russia's ally, France, following the German war plan drawn up by Field Marshal von Schlieffen. Thus the French Empire, stretching from Morocco to Indochina, became involved. So too did her ally Britain and her world-wide empire, drawn in by the double obligation to France as a member of the Triple Entente, and to Belgium whose neutrality von Schlieffen proposed to infringe immediately (despite a guarantee by Germany, France and Britain). Later, Japan, Turkey, Bulgaria, Italy, Romania, Portugal, the United States and many others would be drawn in. The tentacles of the war would stretch across the globe.

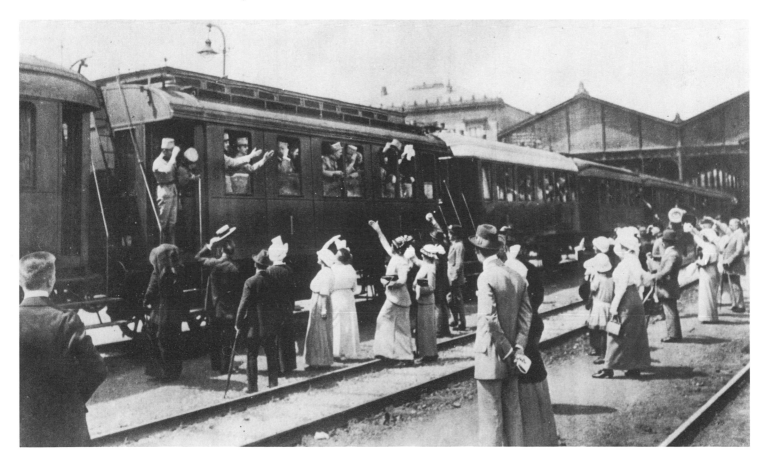

Below: British troops in the
Boer War dig simple
'scrapes' as a defence
against the accuracy of long-
range firepower. The power
of modern weapons upset
the old concept of a war
based on manoeuvre.

Bottom: Artillery was to be
the 'God of war' during
World War I. Here a 15in
howitzer is prepared for
action, Arras, September
1917.

If German militarism set it off, and the alliances shaped it, 20th-century technology gave the war its remorseless and consuming character. Not only were all forms of weapons more deadly than they had ever been before, but the technology of the Industrial Revolutions provided new types of weapon, even new dimensions of war itself – in the air and under the sea.

It was the First Industrial Revolution technology, based on steam (from coal) as a power source and steel and iron as primary materials, which enabled the nations to transport the armies of millions on which all depended to their battlefronts. This was the provenance of the great fleets and merchant marines which carried millions of men and uncounted tons of supplies across the seas, and of the hundreds of thousands of miles of railways on which great steam locomotives drew them to the battle zones.

The Second Industrial Revolution, based on oil as a power source fuelling the internal combustion engine, with light metals and alloys as prime materials, produced aviation as a new dimension. Air reconnaissance (including photography) leading to air combat to obtain air superiority, and short- and long-range bombing all made their first appearances, promising a radical transformation of war itself. On the ground, the internal combustion engine brought about a revolution in transport with the motor lorry and bus, and in communications, with the car and motor bicycle. It also produced first the armoured car, and then an entirely new weapon, the tank.

The battlefields themselves were dominated by firepower, of artillery and automatic weapons. From the very first this was seen to be an artillery war; it was artillery that blasted the Belgian forts in August 1914; artillery played a large part in driving the armies underground into trenches; it inflicted by far the largest number of casualties; it decided the issue of battles. The increasing power and sophistication of artillery was a continuous feature of the war; 'barrages' of different types were evolved for different purposes; sound-ranging and flash-spotting were introduced for counter-battery work; above all, 'predicted shooting' with the aid of accurate maps provided by aerial photography and using the naval practice of calibration restored the element of surprise and made artillery the decisive arm in 1918. Automatic weapons (heavy and light machine guns)

proved to be deadly man-stoppers in open ground with good visibility; one of the most effective counters to them was smoke – delivered by artillery.

Trench warfare itself called for the revival of many ancient practices of siege warfare, and the revival of old weapons, such as trench mortars and grenades (thrown either mechanically or by hand). Chemistry and modern technology provided new versions of other old weapons: fire in the form of flamethrowers, and asphyxiation in the form of various poison gases. At first emitted from containers and at the mercy of the wind, these were later delivered in drums by projectors, and finally with great accuracy at long ranges by the ubiquitous artillery.

Battlefield communications provided examples both of revolutionary advance and of utter frustration. The field telephone became an essential weapon of war, the fronts being stitched together by thousands of miles of cable – always highly vulnerable to shellfire. Meanwhile wireless telegraphy and radio-telephony made great strides. Among their offshoots were radio interception and cryptography, direction-finding and jamming. It had become possible to communicate across great distances, but what technology was not yet ready to offer was the short-range communication essential for battle (provided by the 'walkie-talkie' mobile transmitter-receivers of World War II). World War I was the only war ever fought without voice control, which meant that the generals became quite impotent at the very moment when they would expect and be expected to display their greatest proficiency – the moment when they committed their troops to battle. In this simple fact lay the source of many tragedies, but the overwhelming tragedy was the character imparted to the war by industrial technology, whose remorseless progress would make the next great war an even more devastating experience.

John Terraine

Right: An aerial view of a gas attack on the Eastern Front. Poison gas was only one of a whole new generation of weapons that brought warfare into the industrial age.

Below: Some of the many casualties of a war where mass armies fought with devastatingly powerful weapons. British and German wounded withdraw from the front line during the Battle of the Somme, 19 July 1916.

Chapter 1 The war in the West 1914

Above: General Joseph Joffre, French Commander-in-Chief 1914–16, and victor of the Battle of the Marne.

Below: The Kaiser and the Chief of the General Staff, Colonel-General Helmut von Moltke (right foreground), at German Army manoeuvres.

In August 1914 the Imperial German Army deployed 1,485,000 men on the Western Front, organised into seven armies. Its task was to smash the opposing French forces with the utmost rapidity, and after achieving victory in the west, to turn east to deal with the Russians. According to the Schlieffen Plan, the three large northern armies (750,000 men) would advance through Belgium, thereby outflanking the French, who would be pinned down by the other four German armies acting in a primarily defensive role. Although over-ambitious given the limited forces at the Kaiser's disposal, the Schlieffen Plan was an imaginative attempt to solve Germany's two-front strategic dilemma. Effective Commander-in-Chief of the German Army in this daring enterprise was the Chief of the General Staff, Colonel-General Helmut von Moltke. However, the indecisive and temperamental von Moltke was poorly suited for such a responsibility; he was soon to find himself losing control of his forces when the great advance got under way.

France's grand design to secure victory went under the name of Plan XVII and consisted of a direct advance into Lorraine supported by a subsidiary offensive against Alsace. Plan XVII relied upon the supposed inherent superiority of the offensive; France's military theorists had reduced the role of strategy to the simple transportation of the army to the battlefield, and once in the realm of tactics French *élan* (dash) and *cran* (grit) would carry all before them. Events were to prove otherwise.

Early on the morning of 4 August 1914, advance elements of the German Army crossed the border into neutral Belgian. Although little interference was expected from the Belgian Army (117,000 men strong, under the command of King Albert) the fortresses of Liège and Namur were potential obstacles to the easy transit of German forces through the country. Liège, astride the main route into Belgium, was a special problem, and the German planners had made special provision for its reduction: 30.5cm Skoda and 42cm Krupp super-heavy howitzers reduced the steel and concrete fortifications to rubble in just over a week (8–16 August). General Alexander von Kluck's First Army marched into Brussels on the 20th; the remainder of the Belgian Army retired northward to the fortress system of Antwerp; and on the 21st General Karl von Bülow's Second Army began its investment of Namur.

Meanwhile, General Joseph Joffre, the French Commander-in-Chief, launched Plan XVII. The sideshow in Alsace achieved little. After a series of attacks and counter-attacks, the right flank of General Auguste Dubail's First Army was left clinging on to a small strip of German territory near Mülhausen. The main offensive was spearheaded by the Second Army (General Noël de Castelnau) marching into Lorraine, supported by the remainder of Dubail's troops. Initially the Germans fell back, drawing in the over-confident French; then, on 20 August, Crown Prince Rupprecht's Sixth Army launched a devastating counter-attack – the Battles of Morhange and Sarrebourg – which saw the French thrown back to their own frontier within five days.

Further north, the French fared little better. Their left (the Third and Fourth Armies under General Ruffey and General Fernand de Langle de Cary) attempted an advance into the Ardennes. French reconnaissance was poor, and in a confusing series of engagements they were badly mauled. The offensive was abandoned on 25 August.

General Charles Lanrezac was one of the few French commanders to perceive the intent of the German manoeuvre through Belgium, and he obtained Joffre's permission to extend the French left with his Fifth Army. Alongside his troops was Great Britain's contribution to the land battle, the 110,000 men of the British Expeditionary Force (BEF) under Field Marshal Sir John French.

On 22 August von Kluck's First Army discovered the presence of the BEF, whose II Corps (General Sir Horace Smith-Dorrien) had taken up positions along the Mons–Condé Canal, and next morning the Germans were stopped in their tracks by British rapid

rifle-fire, although German outflanking movements forced the BEF to retire the following day. The French Fifth Army was already in full retreat, and the BEF was forced to fight a number of holding actions, including the costly Battle of Le Cateau, to check the German advance.

By 25 August the Allied position was critical; the French offensives had all failed dismally. The Germans were steadily advancing, and everywhere the French armies were in retreat. At this moment of crisis Joffre's imperturbable resolution saved the situation. With Plan XVII in ruins, he set about reorganising his troops to build a force for a counter-stroke – switching divisions from eastern France by rail to form General Michel Joseph Maunoury's Sixth Army on the extreme Allied left. As a first step he ordered the wavering Lanrezac to counter-attack between Guise and St Quentin. Despite personal reservations Lanrezac conducted the battle with considerable skill: the engagement opened with a French attack towards St Quentin, but the real battle developed in front of Guise, where von Bülow's Second Army pinned down the French right wing. A French counter-attack inflicted a severe check on the Second Army, causing von Bülow to request immediate assistance from von Kluck's army. Instead of swinging around Paris to the west, as planned, the German First Army now altered its direction due south.

The further south the Germans advanced the more exposed their right wing became to a flank attack. By early September Maunoury's army was in place to the north of Paris with the remainder of the French forces south of the River Marne. The military governor of the capital, General Joseph Simon Galliéni, urged that he and Maunoury should launch an attack on von Kluck's flank, to which Joffre agreed, simultaneously ordering an all-out counter-attack along the entire French line.

The Battle of the Marne opened with Maunoury's assault on the German First Army along the River Ourcq. Von Kluck's troops had little difficulty holding the French, but the movement of forces to his right flank opened up a gap between his men and von Bülow's Second Army. The strength of the French counter-attack came as a shock to von Moltke and his army commanders, and when the BEF and the French Fifth Army (now under the energetic leadership of General Louis Franchet d'Esperey) advanced into the gap, German resolution began to waver. On 8 September the Germans began to retire.

The Allied follow-up lacked vigour, however, and allowed the Germans to retreat in good order to the heights overlooking the River Aisne. The arrival of reserve formations bolstered the German line, which held firm in spite of desperate attacks by the French and British on 13 and 14 September. The Germans lost no time in entrenching their positions; they were better equipped for trench warfare than the Allies, and by the end of the month a stalemate had developed. As deadlock extended along the front, both sides commenced a series of outflanking manoeuvres, later dubbed the 'Race to the Sea'. When the opposing armies reached the Belgian coast at Nieuport, a continuous line of battle stretched 725km (450 miles) from the North Sea to Switzerland, and all possibility of turning the flanks disappeared. So died the Schlieffen Plan.

First to pay the price of failure was von Moltke, replaced as Commander-in-Chief by General Erich von Falkenhayn on 14 September. While the battle-lines leap-frogged northwards through France, Ant-werp fell to the Germans on 9 October, and the Belgian Army retired down the coast to join the Allies behind the River Yser. Here the German advance was held by the resolute Belgian defence supported by French troops and Marines; when the Belgians opened the sluice-gates to flood the low-lying country, fighting in this sector died down. Meanwhile, however, another fierce battle had flared up a few kilometres to the southeast, around the ancient town of Ypres.

The First Battle of Ypres marked the last burst of open warfare in the west. One by one the three army corps of the BEF came north from the Aisne to Ypres, together with elements of a fourth corps shipped direct from England, and the advance units of an Indian corps – the first of the British Empire contingents. I Corps, under Lieutenant-General Sir Douglas Haig, arrived on 19 October, just in time to participate in the last Allied attempt to take the offensive. In the face of superior German forces, and especially the very greatly superior German artillery, this came to a swift halt, and thereafter the battle became a grim defensive struggle in which British musketry again played a major role. Both British and French were tried to their limits; losses were very great; but the Germans were halted in front of Ypres. Thus the famous Ypres Salient was born. This battle gravely weakened the British regular army. More important-ly, however, it marked also the end of the war of movement, and for Germany the prospect that she chiefly feared – a long war on two fronts.

Above: Field Marshal Sir John French, commander of the British Expeditionary Force in 1914. Although small in size, the BEF played a decisive role in the Battles of the Marne and Ypres.

Below: Based on the Schlieffen Plan of 1905, the great German advance through northern France.

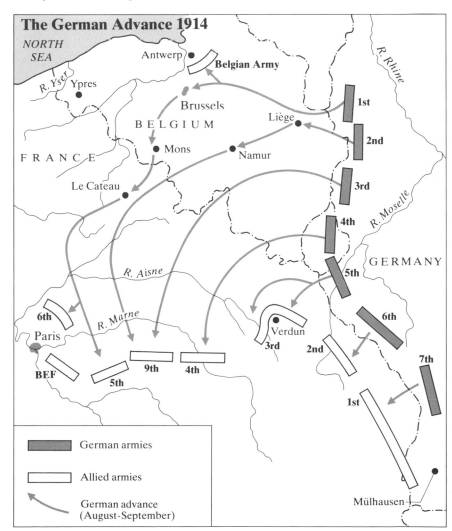

The German Advance 1914

German armies

Allied armies

German advance (August-September)

Europe goes to war
The armies mobilise

1 Dressed in ceremonial uniforms dating back to the age of Frederick the Great, Prussian Foot Guards await inspection. The 'mascot' is the Crown Prince, subsequently an army commander on the Western Front.

2 British officers are instructed in the techniques of machine-gun fire at the School of Musketry, Hythe. In 1914 each infantry battalion was equipped with two Vickers machine guns; a similar ratio was to be found in the German Army.

3 Enthusiastic Viennese crowds celebrate the alliance between Austria-Hungary and Germany as war is declared. The portraits held aloft are of Kaiser Wilhelm and Emperor Franz Joseph.

4 Cheering German troops en route for Belgium in August 1914. The chalked slogans refer to the potency of the 42cm siege howitzer ('Big Bertha') and the intended destination of these troops – Paris.

5 Accepting the farewells of Parisian well-wishers, French cuirassiers depart for the Western Front. Equipped in the style of the Napoleonic era, such troops were not prepared for modern warfare.

6 A group of French infantrymen pose for the camera at a railway depot. Their blue coats and scarlet trousers made them conspicuous targets, a contributory factor in the huge number of French casualties suffered in August 1914.

7 The Kaiser (centre) and Chief of Staff von Moltke (right) confer at the German Army manoeuvres of 1913.

13

Battle of the Frontiers

1 German infantry kneel down at the edge of a wood in expectation of orders to advance. The series of border clashes between France and Germany, which came to be known as the Battle of the Frontiers, cruelly exposed the limitations of the tactical doctrines of 1914.

2 The bayonet charge. Although only a training photograph (from the French Army manoeuvres of July 1914), it graphically reveals the folly of French tactics in 1914: large masses of men in the open made themselves perfect targets for German artillery and machine-gun fire.

3 Escorted by an Alsatian guard dog, men of a French outpost detachment bring their rifles to bear. The 8mm Lebel mle 1886 was the standard infantry weapon of the French Army in 1914. Like other service rifles of the period it had a bolt-action loading system, although an unusual feature was its eight-round tubular magazine housed horizontally below the barrel.

4 A machine-gun section from a French dragoon regiment takes up a firing position. Between the two machine-gun dug-outs is the section officer who, with the aid of binoculars, directs the fire of his men. The French Army deployed vast numbers of cavalry in the opening stages of the Battle of the Frontiers. The main function of cavalry in 1914 was to provide forward reconnaissance and to protect the flanks of the infantry armies. The size of the battlefield in World War I and the physical limitations of the horse made adequate reconnaissance impossible, however, and this role was soon to be taken over by aircraft.

5 Under a hot summer sun German troops advance towards an enemy position. Whereas the professional British Expeditionary Force was fully trained in fieldcraft and minor tactics, the German Army suffered limitations in this area.

6 An artillery officer directs the crew of a 7.7cm FK 96n/A, the standard field gun of the German Army in 1914–15. The FK 96 was not as good as its French equivalent (the famous 'Seventy-five'), but the Germans did enjoy overall superiority in howitzers and heavy artillery.

7 French and German dead lie scattered on the battlefield. The Battle of the Frontiers produced horrifying casualty figures. In the first two weeks of fighting the French lost 210,000 men – a casualty rate greater than that of the Champagne offensives of 1915 or even Verdun.

The fall of Belgium

1 Belgian troops collapse by the roadside in a state of complete exhaustion following their defeat around Louvain on 20 August 1914. The use of dogs for light haulage purposes was a feature of the Belgian armed forces in 1914.

2 German infantry of von Kluck's First Army marches through the centre of Brussels under the gaze of Belgian civilians. The ruthlessness of the German advance through neutral Belgium horrified world opinion. The German Army pursued an official policy of *Schrecklichkeit* ('frightfulness') to cow the Belgian population, thereby avoiding the need to leave large numbers of troops guarding rear communications. Well-documented instances of wholesale destruction and the killing of civilians took place throughout Belgium.

3 Once the Germans had broken through Belgium's frontier defences, the Belgian Army could do little to stem the tide of invasion. Hasty barricades were set up to cover the army's retreat towards Antwerp.

4 German and Austro-Hungarian officers survey the remains of a steel cupola in the fortress of Namur, one of the key elements in Belgium's defensive system. These much-vaunted defences could not stand up to the German 42cm and Austrian 30.5cm siege howitzers.

5 Anachronistically dressed Belgian troops line a roadway in expectation of a German attack. The Belgian Army of 1914 was caught in a state of transition, converting from an essentially volunteer force to a full conscript army along modern lines.

6 Firing 7.65mm FN mle 1889 rifles (based on the German Mauser pattern), a Belgian rearguard defends a canal bridge during the retreat to Antwerp. Stiff Belgian resistance and the demolition of bridges and railway tunnels aimed to slow the German advance, but gained little time for the French to re-deploy their forces for the Battle of the Marne.

The great retreat
France in danger

1 British troops come under artillery fire from German field guns. An air-burst shrapnel round has just exploded; while horses stampede and men run for cover, an officer (second from right) clasps his hands to a head-wound.

2 Good communications were an essential prerequisite for the control of the mass armies of 1914. Radio-telegraphy was in its infancy, so recourse had to be made to more primitive methods, such as these French carrier pigeons.

3 Armed with .303in SMLE (No 1 Mark III) rifles, two British infantrymen advance cautiously alongside a hedge during the opening phases of the conflict. At the Battles of Mons and Le Cateau the small BEF inflicted severe checks on the Germans, but being unable to secure its flanks, it had to retire. The German First Army pressed onward with great resolution, continually pressurising the exhausted British troops.

4 A weary file of British infantrymen trudges through a field in Belgium. The retreat from Mons was an unforgettable ordeal for the survivors of the battles of 1914; long forced marches interspersed with bitter rearguard actions against the advancing Germans.

5 A squadron of German dragoons awaits the order to advance. Like their French counterparts the German cavalry failed to provide adequate information of enemy movements. On a number of occasions the Germans were unaware that they were facing the BEF.

6 German field artillery advances along a dusty road in northern France, September 1914. The German commanders pushed their men to the limits, especially von Kluck, whose First Army covered vast distances in August and September, causing problems of supply and communication.

Battle of the Marne
The Allied counter-attack

1 The Battle of the Marne involved a massive movement of French forces, and any means of transport was pressed into service to get the men to the battlefield. Here British omnibuses and trucks, loaned to the French, are made ready.

2 The famous French 'Seventy-five' in action during the Battle of the Marne. To the left of the gun is the limber holding up to 80 spare rounds, a supply that was quickly exhausted under battlefield conditions, given the gun's exceptional rate-of-fire of 20 rounds per minute. On the ladder an observer plots the fall of shot.

3 A column of German prisoners is led away under an escort of French cuirassiers.

4 Under the gaze of the local priest, a battalion of French infantry marches through a village near the Marne battlefield. The well-ordered and rapid redeployment of forces by the French General Staff was an important factor in the Allied victory.

5 The German retreat from the Marne stopped on the hills overlooking the River Aisne, where this machine-gun detachment is setting up. The 7.92mm Maxim was the standard machine gun of the German Army during the war, and like the British Vickers was a water-cooled weapon capable of sustained fire at long ranges. Its weakness was its weight – 62kg (136lb) compared to 40kg (88lb) for the Vickers – although this was less important in the defensive operations soon to be adopted by the Germans on the Western Front.

6 A mixed group of French officers observes the German retreat from the Marne. The officer in the centre is from a dragoon regiment; his burnished steel and brass helmet is fitted with a cloth cover as a concession to camouflage.

7 A French infantry section, armed with Lebel rifles, guards a canal bank. During September 1914 the French began to adopt more cautious tactics.

First Battle of Ypres

1 The First Battle of Ypres (12 October to 11 November 1914) consisted of a series of engagements; determined German attacks were followed by equally resolute Allied counter-attacks. These infantrymen hold an improvised breastwork in a wood to the east of Ypres. The German drive to achieve a breakthrough before the trench line solidified stretched the Allies to the utmost and promoted a new spirit of cooperation between the French and British.

2 Men of the Oxford and Bucks Light Infantry rest behind their brigade HQ at the height of the battle.

3 German gunners at a covered artillery post in the Ypres sector. The Germans had a great advantage over the Allies, both in numbers and calibre of ordnance.

4 As the trench system developed, so too did the digging of mines as a means of destroying enemy fortifications. Here a mine is detonated on the Ypres Salient.

5 A gun-crew of the Royal Field Artillery fuzes and loads shells for an 18-pounder field gun. This reliable weapon was to see service in all theatres during the course of the war.

momentum, largely through shortages of supplies and munitions, and General August von Mackensen's counter-attack around Lodz (18–25 November) pushed the Russians back to the Vistula.

In 1915 the stalemate in the west and the plight of the Austrians forced General von Falkenhayn to adopt a new strategy – a major effort against Russia. Fighting of a most desperate nature took place all winter in sub-zero temperatures in the Carpathians, but the first important move came in February 1915 with an unsuccessful German offensive from East Prussia.

The main offensive came further south in Galicia, along the line Gorlice–Tarnow. A newly formed Eleventh Army under von Mackensen was secretly brought up and a short bombardment of unprecedented weight on 2 May began the advance in the central sector. The German breakthrough caught the Russians completely by surprise, and was rapidly followed by a carefully planned exploitation. In only two weeks the Germans advanced over 130km (80 miles) and by the end of the month the Eleventh Army alone had taken 153,000 prisoners. The Russians began to fall back along their entire front and Warsaw fell on 4 August; three weeks later Brest-Litovsk was in German hands. The Austro-German advance continued into September, but then petered out, and as the Russians at last recovered a new front line was formed.

The Austro-German forces had made massive gains: they had advanced nearly 500km (300 miles) and had inflicted an estimated 2,000,000 casualties on the Russians. To any other nation such a defeat would have been a mortal blow; Russia, however, not only survived but accelerated the expansion of her war industries, began to build up military supplies, and by the following year was even considering offensive operations.

In the south, Serbia remained a thorn in the flank of the Central Powers throughout 1915, and when they signed a treaty with Bulgaria on 6 September 1915 plans were drawn up to destroy the Serbian irritant for good. General von Mackensen was sent to direct the combined Austro-German-Bulgarian forces. In October the Austro-German armies invaded Serbia from the north while two Bulgarian armies struck across her border in the east. Outnumbered and outflanked, the Serbs – soldiers and civilians together – were forced to retreat westward through the mountains of Albania. British and French forces landed at Salonika in Greece, but their advance was successfully barred by the Bulgarians. Anglo-French troopships were sent to pick up the survivors of the gruelling march through the Albanian mountains, but this was the only help the western powers could offer their Balkan ally, and consequently 1915 saw the end of 'plucky little Serbia'.

Above left: Colonel-General August von Mackensen. One of the most able of Germany's generals, von Mackensen scored a major success over the Russians at Gorlice–Tarnow in May 1915.

Above: Colonel-General Conrad von Hötzendorf, the Austrian Chief-of-Staff. His grandiose plans in Galicia were turned into a massive defeat for the Austrian Army, August–September 1914.

Children of the Tsar
The Russian Army in 1914

1 The backbone of the Imperial Russian Army: massed infantry drawn from the Russian peasantry. The numerical strength of the Tsar's army was impressive: over a million men in peacetime, rising to four million after full mobilisation.

2 The Russian 76.2mm field gun was a good artillery piece – easily the equal of the German 77mm – but shell shortages and old-fashioned artillery tactics greatly reduced its effectiveness.

3 Armed with 7.62mm Mosin-Nagant rifles, Russian infantrymen wait in a trench in Galicia during fighting against the Austrians.

4 A Russian machine-gun motorcycle combination training in an anti-aircraft role in 1914. The 7.62mm PM1910 was a direct copy of the German Maxim machine gun, a reliable weapon highly regarded by Russia's German opponents.

5 A supply wagon arrives at a forward position to distribute smallarms ammunition to front-line infantry. The Russian Army of World War I was one of contrast: on the one hand it was bedevilled by bureaucratic ineptitude, but on the other its weapons and equipment were of a generally high standard.

6 The Tsar of all the Russias (saluting) and the army's Commander-in-Chief, Grand Duke Nicholas (centre), inspect an infantry regiment. After the defeats of 1915 the Tsar took over direct control of the armed forces, but his weak and vacillating leadership was to prove disastrous.

7 Wearing distinctive headgear, Russian cossacks pause in a forest clearing near the front line. Despite their famous cavalry tradition, they performed poorly in their allotted reconnaissance role. The war on the Eastern Front was fought over vast distances, and all the combatant armies had major problems in gaining intelligence on the enemy's dispositions.

Tannenberg
The battle for Prussia

1 From a well-entrenched position – shored-up with pine logs and utilising steel firing plates – German infantry look across to Russian positions in the Masurian Lakes region of East Prussia. Although greatly outnumbered, the screen of German troops facing General Rennenkampf's army had little trouble in holding their ground. Rennenkampf inexplicably failed to follow up his initial victory at Gumbinnen and did nothing to come to the aid of General Samsonov, whose army was being annihilated at Tannenberg.

2 Rays of sunlight stream through the windows of a church in Russian Poland, commandeered by the Germans as a temporary billet for their men. Unlike his Russian counterpart, the German soldier was relatively well-cared for.

3 German troops march through the pine forests of East Prussia, en route to encircle the unwieldy Russian forces. The superiority of the German Army allowed its commanders to take on huge numbers of Russians with every prospect of success.

4 A home-from-home: German infantrymen relax in an entrenchment on the Eastern Front in 1914. Photographs such as this were widely distributed in Germany, providing soldiers' families with a reassuring picture of life at the front.

5 On the other hand, this remarkable photograph shows the reality of war, as Russian troops come under artillery fire. Samsonov's Second Army was destroyed in the four-day Battle of Tannenberg.

6 Equipped with lances, men of the 2nd Prussian Cavalry Division advance into Poland. After Tannenberg the main role for German cavalry was to guard the masses of Russian prisoners.

Lemberg
Defeat for Austria

1 A Hungarian cavalryman negotiates a ditch, Galicia, 1914. Besides the German-speaking forces (mainly from Austria) the Hungarians were the only reliable troops in the polyglot Austro-Hungarian Empire.

2 The main battleground between Austria and Russia was the province of Galicia, which the Austrians protected with a series of complex defences. Here troops race forward with wire mattresses and trestles to help buttress a forward field fortification against Russian attack.

3 Piles of Hungarian dead litter a battlefield near Lemberg, after one of a series of defeats for Austria-Hungary at the hands of the Russians. Overall casualties were enormous: as many as 400,000 by the end of September 1914 and over 1,000,000 by the end of the year. Austria-Hungary was never to recover from these disasters; the formerly mighty empire was firmly on the road to disintegration.

4 Supported by a fire-group in a roadside ditch, Austrian infantrymen race forward to attempt to take a position during the bloody fighting for Lemberg.

5 An Austrian machine-gun crew defending an artillery emplacement in the Carpathians prepares for an enemy attack. The 8mm Schwarzlose Model 07/12 machine gun equipped Austria's armies throughout the war.

6 The pride of the Austrian heavy artillery: the 30.5cm Skoda M1911 howitzer. Weighing 20,830kg (45,922lb), this giant howitzer could lob a 382kg (842lb) shell to a range of 9600m (10,500yd), and was capable of smashing through the strongest concrete emplacements. In this photograph the gun has just been fired; the cradle-hoist (left of gun) is empty but ready to take the shell just behind the gun. Spare shells lie in line within wooden casings under a camouflage of branches. As well as being used on the Eastern Front, a number of these howitzers were deployed to destroy the Belgian forts in 1914 and at Verdun in 1916.

Serbia at war

1 A Serbian machine-gun crew in action during the summer of 1914. Evidence of Serbia's connections with her fellow-Slavs in Russia is the Russian-made 7.62mm PM1910 machine gun, set up here in the sustained-fire role. Unlike the Austrian enemy, the Serbian Army was a cohesive force, highly motivated in the defence of its homeland and with fighting experience gained in the two recent Balkan Wars. It was, however, chronically short of modern weapons. Strenuous efforts were therefore made to buy hardware from friendly nations, which led to a multiplicity of weapon types and problems with ammunition supply.

2 A heavily armed and armoured monitor of Austria's Danube Flotilla being made ready for action. The first shots of World War I were fired by vessels of this kind, when Austria bombarded the Serbian capital of Belgrade on 29 July 1914.

3 Austro-Hungarian troops sit by the camp fire during their disastrous campaign against the Serbs in the autumn of 1914. The soldier on the right is a sergeant in the Hungarian Gendarmerie.

4 Undaunted by the shells bursting in front of them, Serbian troops charge forward to attack the Austrians in the great counter-offensive of 3–15 December 1914. This operation drove the enemy from Serbian soil, and over 40,000 prisoners and 133 guns fell into Serbian hands.

5 The Serbian Commander-in-Chief, Marshal Putnik, reviews his men on horseback. Putnik was a most able commander, employing his meagre forces to the utmost effect.

6 Serbian civilians – both women and men – are hanged with military precision by Austro-Hungarian forces in Mačva, 1914. General Potiorek, the Austrian commander, instigated a ruthless punitive campaign against the Serbian population; hostages were taken as a matter of course and any sign of civil disobedience led to immediate executions.

The winter war
Eastern Front 1914-15

1 German cavalrymen advance towards Augustowo during the Winter Battle in Masuria. Fought in a near-continuous blizzard during January 1915, the Germans achieved a considerable local tactical success (capturing 100,000 Russians) without, however, influencing the overall strategic position on the Eastern Front.

2 The railway system was the key element in the Austro-German superiority of strategic mobility. Troop transport was a top priority, and every effort was made to keep the lines open and the trains running.

3 Pushed back by the Russians out of Galicia, the Austrians fought a desperate battle to hold the mountain passes over the Carpathians. These Austrian troops are keeping a careful watch from an outpost high in the mountains.

4 Although a highly posed photograph – typical of this period of the war – this nonetheless shows an interesting array of weaponry and equipment employed by the German Army in 1914–15. On the left a field telephone is being used; an officer looks through a rangefinder (centre); and on the right, a gun-crew loads a 24.5cm trench mortar (*Minenwerfer*). This was a fearsome infantry weapon, firing a heavy, high-angle shell to a maximum range of 550m (600yd) at a rate-of-fire of up to 20 rounds per minute.

5/6 Various attempts were made to defend the valuable and vulnerable infantryman against the destructive fire of quick-firing rifles and machine guns. One of the most bizarre was this contraption, invented in Austria. A complex system of interlocking plates gave some protection to the soldier while advancing (**5**) and even allowed him to fire his rifle from cover (**6**). Not surprisingly this cumbersome device saw only limited service.

7 A Russian 280mm heavy howitzer in its emplacement outside the walls of the besieged Austrian fortress of Przemysl. The great fortress was invested on 1 November 1914 and finally fell to the Russians on 22 March 1915.

Gorlice-Tarnow
The Germans break through

1 In 1915 the Germans transferred their main strategic effort to the Eastern Front. Their aim was to knock Russia out of the war; how this was to be achieved led to heated exchanges between Generals von Falkenhayn and Ludendorff. Despite this, at the tactical level German preparations were characteristically thorough. In this photograph German soldiers practise an important battlefield technique – cutting through barbed-wire defences.

2 German troops train with rifle-grenades in Poland. Rifle-grenades could be effective in trench warfare when used en masse, but their lack of range and accuracy led to their withdrawal in 1916.

3 Poison gas was first used (ineffectually, however) on the Eastern Front at Bolimov in Poland on 31 January 1915. As gas was a notoriously double-edged weapon these German infantrymen on the Eastern Front wear rudimentary gas masks as protection against a gas blow-back.

4 The German breakthrough between Gorlice and Tarnow was a major achievement but more important was the brilliant exploitation of the initial success. All German commanders were instructed to push their troops to the utmost, regardless of any physical obstacles.

5 This photograph sums up the state of Austro-German relations in 1915. German troops (left) march towards the battlefront, while soldiers of their Austrian ally (right) look on as bystanders.

6 During 1915 the Germans captured an estimated 1,000,000 Russian prisoners. Here several thousand of them wait at a transit point in Augustowo before transportation to POW camps.

Serbia in defeat

1 Bulgarian troops adopt firing positions in a simple slit trench. As soon as Bulgaria entered the war on the side of the Central Powers (on 11 October 1915) Serbia's fate was sealed. Faced by the Austro-Germans to the north, the opening of her long eastern border to Bulgarian attack placed Serbia in an untenable strategic position.

2 Assault troops of the 11th Bavarian Infantry Division cross the River Danube on 7 October 1915, the first phase of the destruction of Serbia. Under the overall control of Field-Marshal von Mackensen (the victor of Gorlice–Tarnow), combined Austrian and German armies attacked Serbia from the north.

3 An Austrian firing-squad deals summarily with Serbian prisoners. Such measures were viewed by the Austrians as revenge for the murder of Archduke Franz Ferdinand by Serbian nationalists at Sarajevo in June 1914.

4 Faced by overwhelming odds the Serbs were forced to retreat, but they refused to surrender. The Serbian High Command made the decision to conduct a fighting withdrawal through the mountains to Albania, where the navies of Britain and Italy could transport them to a base at Corfu. Here, in harsh conditions, the Serbian rearguard makes a stand near the Albanian border.

5 In good order, a long line of Serbian troops winds its way across the snowy wastes, and disappears over the horizon. Despite all their problems, the Serbs managed to transport 25,000 Austrian prisoners to a new captivity beyond the Balkans.

6 Pulled by oxen, a Serbian supply column struggles towards safety. Besides being pursued by the Bulgarian Army, the cold and exhausted Serbs fell victim to an outbreak of typhus which further decimated their ranks.

Chapter 3

Trench stalemate in the West

As the conflict entered its second year, hopes that it would be a short war ('It'll all be over by Christmas' was a common catchphrase of 1914) were replaced by preparations for a long haul. In the west the strategic initiative lay with Germany: her armies were in possession of Belgium and France's industrial centres in the north, standing, as General Joffre said: 'a mere five days' march from the heart of France. This situation made it clear to every Frenchman that our task consisted in defeating this enemy, and driving him out of our country.' When it became clear that the Germans were transferring substantial forces from west to east, the opportunity arose for the Allies to undertake large offensives. This remained their strategic imperative throughout the year. All that was lacking was the means.

The British Expeditionary Force was steadily expanding, yet Britain remained the junior partner in the coalition and French strategy predominated. The price that Britain was going to have to pay for her involvement in European politics now became apparent: hitherto primarily a sea power, she now had to raise a mass army for continental war. In 1914, the only backing for her small regular army was the Territorial Force, intended for home defence. To remedy this state of affairs, Lord Kitchener, Secretary of State for War, issued his famous appeal for volunteers, and by the end of the year 1,186,357 men had responded. By the time voluntary recruiting dried up, the 'Kitchener Armies' totalled an astonishing 3,621,045 men – and the military authorities faced the daunting logistical problem of equipping and training them for the field.

There arose, furthermore, the question, 'which field?' Some British politicians were shocked by the unprecedented casualty lists from France and Flanders, and the obvious stalemate in the west. They looked to sea power as a means of opening up fronts elsewhere, where the new recruits might be more profitably employed. From 1915 onwards there was to be a frequently bitter argument among British strategists between the 'Westerners', who saw that the main and decisive front was in the west, and the 'Easterners', who urged attacks on Austria or Turkey. For most of 1915, however, the remnants of the Old Army, including units drawn from garrisons overseas, held the line in the west, supported by some Territorials and contingents from India and Canada.

General Joffre defined the essential problem facing the Allied commanders as 'a race between our offensive matériel and the German defensive organisations'. By the spring of 1915 the Germans had constructed a complex trench network protected by barbed wire and backed by machine guns that greatly increased the power of the defence.

Western Front trench systems varied considerably according to the underlying terrain, but typically consisted of a winding, front-line fire trench, traversed to avoid enfilade fire, out of which ran a series of saps towards the enemy position which provided 'jumping-off' points for an assault or ended in listening-posts. Behind the fire-trench ran two or more support lines – where the main body of front-line troops would be stationed – connected to each other by a series of communication trenches dug in a zig-zag pattern. As the war continued, trench systems on both sides became deeper and more complicated. In very wet areas they had to be built up above the ground by using innumerable sandbags. In mountainous districts (the Vosges, for example) they were tunnelled out of rock. The Germans, normally on the defensive, showed particular ingenuity, making good use of the mining and digging equipment that had originally been intended for laying siege to fortresses, and later using ferro-concrete on a lavish scale to construct deep dugouts and 'pill-boxes'.

Against the ever-strengthening trench lines, the Allies tried to seize back the initiative they had lost at the opening of the war. However, they lacked trench-warfare weapons and supplies – everything from trench mortars and grenades to pumps and duckboards – as well as heavy artillery, and were always short of ammunition. The 'Winter Battle in Champagne', lasting from December 1914 to March 1915, cost the French heavy casualties for small gains. The British, even less well-equipped and far weaker in numbers than their allies, could do little to help, and the resulting strain on the coalition was serious.

It was largely to counteract the ill effects of this that the British launched their attack at Neuve Chapelle in

Below: By November 1914 the front line on the Western Front had been established, and over the ensuing months the combatant nations developed the complex trench system which was to remain virtually unchanged until the German withdrawal to the Hindenburg Line in the spring of 1917.
Throughout 1915 the Allies battered themselves against the German defences in vain, and suffered vast casualties.

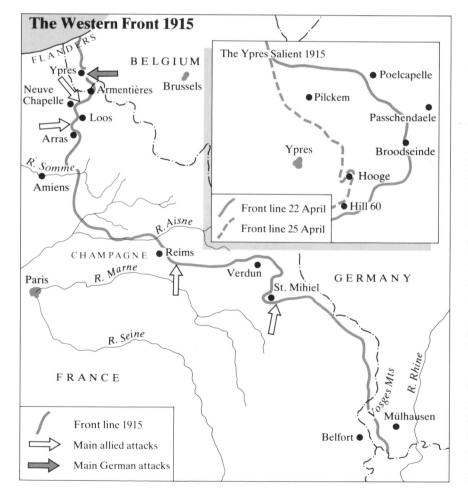

The Western Front 1915

FLANDERS

BELGIUM

Ypres
Neuve Chapelle
Armentières
Brussels
Loos
Arras

R. Somme
Amiens

R. Aisne

CHAMPAGNE — Reims
R. Marne
Paris — Verdun
St. Mihiel — GERMANY

R. Seine

FRANCE

Vosges Mts
R. Rhine
Mülhausen
Belfort

Front line 1915
Main allied attacks
Main German attacks

The Ypres Salient 1915

Poelcapelle
Pilckem
Passchendaele
Ypres
Broodseinde
Hooge
Hill 60

Front line 22 April
Front line 25 April

March. The BEF was now divided into two Armies: First (General Haig), and Second (General Smith-Dorrien); Haig's army was entrusted with this offensive. The preparations were carried out with methodical care; they contained a number of important innovations which made the ensuing battle a blueprint of the trench warfare of the next three years – photographic reconnaissance from the air provided maps of the opposing trenches, artillery timetables were introduced, gun-platforms were constructed to give stability in soft ground, and a short 'hurricane' bombardment was tried out; the infantry were rehearsed in their tasks, and secrecy was carefully preserved. The result was a notable initial success, and then, as a staff officer said, 'the whole machine clogged and stopped. It was maddening.' Furthermore, this would continue to be the maddening pattern of the future.

The time was now approaching for the great Austro-German offensive in the east. To divert Allied attention and mask their real plan, the Germans launched their only western attack of 1915 – the Second Battle of Ypres. On 22 April, after some heavy shelling, a bluish-white mist was seen drifting towards the Allied line on the north side of the Ypres Salient. This was a cloud of chlorine gas, discharged from cylinders against a section of front held by an Algerian and a French Territorial division. Those who inhaled it in quantity died extremely painful deaths; the remainder fled in panic, many choking and gasping. A dangerous gap appeared in the Allied line, but the Germans themselves were hesitant about entering it; it was 'papered over' by a thin screen of Canadian and British troops, and what might have been an outright disaster for the Allies turned into yet another trench warfare slogging-match which continued into May with high casualties on both sides. The Salient was narrowed, and became a more unhealthy place than ever, but it remained in being.

May was the month of the great eastern offensive of the Central Powers; it was also a month of deceptive hope for the Allies. Italy declared war on Austria-Hungary on 23 May, and began a series of offensives in the Alps and along the River Isonzo in the direction of Trieste. The Italians attacked with great dash and enthusiasm, but one by one these offensives (11 along the Isonzo alone) failed, with nothing to show but minimal gains of ground and heavy losses of men. All parts of the Austro-Hungarian Empire fought with fierce determination against Italy. These battles, in 1916 and 1917, supplied some of the grimmest examples of attrition of the war.

Heavy losses continued to be the characteristic of the Western Front. May saw the resumption of the French offensives, this time in Artois under the direction of General Ferdinand Foch. This battle (Second Artois) was a significant milestone of the war: the French used 1252 guns and howitzers, 293 of them heavy; their six-day preliminary bombardment used no fewer than 2,155,862 shells – and this, too, was the pattern of the future. On the first day of the infantry battle (9 May) the French made a dramatic advance almost to the crest of the Vimy Ridge, but their reserves were too far back to exploit it. Once more what had seemed a promising opportunity degenerated into trench attack and counter-attack. The battle continued in this fashion until 18 June, at a cost of over 100,000 French casualties and at least 75,000 Germans. British attempts to give support to the French left failed dismally, due to a desperate shortage of guns, especially the heavy calibres, and ammunition.

Public concern at the ammunition shortage, whipped up by the Press, led to the fall of the Liberal government, the formation of a coalition ministry, and the creation of a new office, the Ministry of Munitions, which, although ineffective at first, later became a valuable instrument for the conduct of the war.

The summer months saw a lull in the major battles, while the French built up the quantities of guns and ammunition that were now essential in what had become an 'artillery war', and the British painfully tried to do the same. By late September all was ready; on the 25th the French attacked again in Champagne with 35 divisions and in Artois with 18; these were supported by 2000 heavy and 3000 field guns – 30 heavy guns per kilometre in Champagne, 22 per kilometre in Artois. It seemed to be an irresistible accumulation of force, and it certainly struck the Germans a heavy blow (25,000 prisoners and 150 guns were captured). But French losses in the two offensives mounted to over 190,000, and the German lines remained unbroken. The British, attacking on the left of the French again, at Loos, used gas for the first time (with a notable lack of success), and were, as ever, short of artillery – only 12 heavy guns to the kilometre. Whereas the French on their right failed on this occasion by having their reserves too close up, so that they were caught by German artillery, the British repeated the French error of 9 May and held their reserves too far back. The result was that early gains were soon lost, and the battle settled down to the all-too-familiar trench fighting, in which losses mounted to 48,267. The first reserves were Kitchener Army divisions, quite inexperienced and somewhat disorganised; for them it was a minor disaster. There was deep dissatisfaction with the result of Britain's largest battle so far. Field Marshal French was removed, and succeeded as Commander-in-Chief of the Expeditionary Force by General Haig.

1915 had proved, for both sides, to be a year of disappointment, with success often tantalisingly close, but never within reach. On the Western Front, technology was the dominant factor, reflected in the increasing use of artillery and the sophistication of artillery techniques. Bombardments became increasingly scientific, with the introduction of new methods such as sound-ranging and flash-spotting, and ever-improving communications with the aircraft that were now seen as essential for this style of war. What no one could yet see was any way of avoiding the churning-up of ground in an artillery battle to such an extent that infantry and supporting guns could not move across it. Worse still, every step of technological progress was matched by a counter-step; in that fact lay the frustration and tragedy of the static phase of the war.

Above left: Field Marshal Sir John French and General Ferdinand Foch. While Foch rose to become overall commander of the Allied armies on the Western Front, French was dismissed at the end of 1915.

Above: Colonel-General Erich von Falkenhayn replaced von Moltke as German Chief-of-Staff and directed German strategy during 1915.

Below: Lord Kitchener, Britain's Secretary of State for War, was one of the few soldiers to realise that the war would be long and bloody.

Trench warfare
The armies dig in

1 German troops aim their rifles through box firing ports in a firing bay of an entrenchment of 1915; the soldier (second right) is just about to load a clip of ammunition into his magazine. This is a fairly simple trench, typical of the period, in which the soil dug out from the trench covers the sandbag parapet at the front and helps make the parados to the rear. Little attempt has been made to shore up the trench and consequently any spell of bad weather would collapse the sides and render it virtually useless.

2 A French infantry unit manning an advanced trench on the Lorraine front. As a general principle, the French paid little attention to their forward trenches, employing them as piquet lines, sparsely manned and of simple construction. The main defences were some distance to the rear.

3 A German fatigue party in the process of trench building in the Argonne, November 1915. The underlying geology of the region dictated the style and construction of the entrenchments, from the sandbag trenches of Flanders to outposts cut into the rock in the Vosges.

4 A trench in a French sector of the line, broadly similar in construction to that in Photograph 1, although an attempt has been made to shore up the trench with wickerwork fencing, a common material in the Argonne. These troops are armed with both hand and rifle grenades – an early attempt to provide the infantryman with greater firepower.

5 A listening post by Vimy Ridge, December 1915. The soldier at the end of the line is using a periscope (covered with sacking for camouflage).

6 Men of the Royal Scots Fusiliers in trenches at La Boutillerie, winter 1914–15. Duckboards have been laid on the trench floor and rifles are at the ready in sandbag loopholes.

War in the Vosges

1 Throughout the war the main centres of conflict on the Western Front lay along the line from the North Sea to Verdun. The line south of Verdun remained relatively quiet, possessing no features of any great strategic importance. The Vosges Mountains, however, witnessed repeated struggles for the region's mountain summits. Specially trained mountain units were the main fighting element in the Vosges, and in this photograph German *Alpenjäger* pose with captured *chasseurs alpins*.

2 A French artilleryman loads a shell into the breech of a 75mm field gun. In order to provide a higher angle of fire (an important factor in mountain warfare) the gun has been mounted on a platform of pine logs. A *chasseur* in traditional blue uniform and large beret can be seen standing to the right of the gun.

3 Alpine troops ski across snow-covered fields in the *Région du Collet* in the Vosges. In winter, conditions could resemble those encountered by the Italians and Austrians in the Alps.

4 A French mountain soldier, wearing winter uniform and equipment. A sheepskin coat (reversed) is worn over a standard uniform, while special overboots/gaiters protect feet and legs.

5 Besides the *chasseur alpin* units the French Army also deployed battalions of *chasseurs à pied* – the equivalent of light infantry. This soldier wears the new-style uniform and is armed with the standard French Army 8mm Lebel rifle with its sword-bayonet already fixed.

6 A German machine-gun crew takes up a position in a snow-filled shell crater in one of the more fought-over areas of the Vosges sector. Although their ordinary headgear makes them easily visible against the snow, they wear white camouflage overalls. Towards the end of the war, winter camouflage clothing and equipment had become fairly commonplace along the Western Front. This 7.92mm Maxim machine gun is fitted with a small shield, clearly of limited use here but originally intended as a guard when firing through specially designed machine-gun loopholes.

France's colonial troops

1 During the 19th century France had built up a large colonial empire in Africa, and small numbers of native troops were brought over to France to supplement her reserves of manpower. These *spahis marocains* gathered round a campfire form the light cavalry element of the Moroccan Division.

2 Newly arrived Senegalese *spahis* on parade provide a fascinating touch of exotica for the local population. Until 1914 such troops had rarely been seen in France.

3 Senegalese riflemen (*tirailleurs*) at an award-giving ceremony. Besides wearing exotic uniforms, France's colonial troops gained a reputation for *élan* in battle – which also earned them a high casualty rate.

4 Colonial troops surge forward out of the trenches through a ripening wheatfield towards the distant enemy. These men are from one of the four regiments of 'Turcos', Algerians who were kitted out in the Turkish-style uniform which had been popular in France during the late 19th century.

5 A French officer reads out a communiqué to his *spahis* near Châlons, 20 July 1915. In colonial regiments, while the men would normally be drawn from native stock, their officers would be French nationals.

6 An Algerian trooper holds the bridle of his Arabian horse, complete with finely tooled leather saddle furniture. As with the regular French cavalry, there were no opportunities for the dashing charges that were the apotheosis of the cavalryman.

7 Uniformed in a more prosaic but more practical French Army uniform, these Senegalese troops arrive in France at St Raphael, Var, on 18 June 1916. During the first two years of the war the French made limited use of their colonies, but, as their own reserves began to dwindle after 1916, increasing numbers of colonial troops were committed to the fray. Large numbers of African troops were involved in the Nivelle offensive of 1917.

Frustration and failure
The French offensives of 1915

1 A tableau of French infantrymen, revealing the new *horizon bleu* uniform which came into service in 1915 to replace the conspicuous scarlet and blue outfit. Headgear consists of the *Adrian* steel helmet, brought into service as a means of protecting the infantry from the blast of shrapnel and high explosive. By 1915 the armies of the main combatant nations had begun the process of re-equipping their forces to face the special problems of trench warfare.

2 A French 75mm field gun fires upon enemy positions, its barrel at the point of maximum recoil. Both gun and limber have been fitted into purpose-built emplacements. The famous 'Seventy-five' had a maximum range of 11,000m (12,030yd) and fired a 6.2kg (13.7lb) shell. This was a relatively lightweight shell for a field gun of this period and the one major weakness of this otherwise fine weapon.

3 An old 155mm gun is re-sited during a bombardment in support of the offensive in Artois, May 1915. Because they were desperately short of large-calibre guns, the French had to use obsolescent fortress artillery.

4 A regimental band leads a column of French infantry marching through a village in northern France in 1915.

5/6 These two action photographs show a French assault against a German position while under heavy fire. French losses during 1915 were enormous: 400,000 men were lost in the offensive in Flanders and Artois during May; the September assault in Champagne cost 145,000 with a further 50,000 from the subsidiary attack in Artois. By the end of 1915 the grim total was 1,961,687 casualties.

Gas attack!
Second Battle of Ypres

1 Soldiers from a Scottish regiment look across no man's land from their trenches within the Ypres Salient.

2 French and British troops share a dug-out in trenches around Zillebeke. The French Army played an important role in the Second Battle of Ypres.

3 The Second Battle of Ypres became notorious for the first successful gas attack; after this the threat of gas became an everyday, though life-and-death, fact of trench existence. Here a spent shell casing is set up as an improvised gas alarm.

4 Taken from a newly captured German position, this photograph shows men of the 1/10th King's Regiment taking cover under the parapet of the trench.

5 The use of poison gas at Ypres prompted rapid counter-measures from the Allies. The French were quick to set up a 'Gas School' where troops were instructed how to protect themselves.

6 German troops with primitive gas masks stand guard in a heavily sandbagged trench. Following its use at Ypres gas warfare developed rapidly: the British first used gas at Loos in October 1915; phosgene made its appearance in December 1915, followed by mustard gas in 1917. Improvements were also made in the techniques of 'delivery', and gas shells replaced the old, unreliable tube dischargers.

7 Men of the Argyll and Sutherland Highlanders wearing improvised gas masks issued on 3 May 1915. The first attempts at countering the gas threat consisted of a wad of material soaked in urine and pressed over the face.

Front-line deadlock
The French Army in defence

1 A salvo of rifle-fire raises dust as French troops fire out from a freshly dug trench in the chalk downlands of northeastern France.

2 A wounded French soldier is helped down a wooded slope by his comrades. Despite the massive casualties suffered by the French Army in 1915, the morale of the troops held firm.

3 The dead lie on stretchers in a barn somewhere in France awaiting burial, August 1915. Whereas the armies of Britain and Germany made strenuous efforts to set up a comprehensive medical service to deal with the hundreds of thousands of wounded which resulted from a major offensive, the French initially lagged behind. Often the ordinary soldier could expect to receive only the most rudimentary medical aid, and this could dwindle to nothing during a major push.

4 The well-ordered trench lines of Flanders and the Somme regions became fragmented in the hills of the Argonne. These French dug-outs are situated on a reverse slope some distance from the forward line.

5 Before the introduction of the standard French steel helmet during 1915 (the *Adrian* pattern) steel skull-caps were issued to the troops to wear under their *képis*. Curiously, this infantryman is wearing his over the *képi*.

6 French wounded are dragged down a narrow trench in the Argonne after falling victim to a German artillery bombardment.

7 A French front-line trench facing Vimy Ridge, October 1915. Thousands of French lives were lost in the battle for this feature; it took the courageous Canadian assault of April 1917 to gain Vimy Ridge permanently for the Allies.

Italy joins the Allies

1 Italy declared war on Austria-Hungary on 23 May 1915, and these soldiers echo the enthusiasm of those who went to war in August 1914. The poster on the freight car door suggests a highly optimistic itinerary, from the home station of Bologna to the enemy capitals of Vienna and Berlin. Also included is Trieste, then an Austrian city but one long-claimed by the Italians.

2 The original caption for this photograph reads: 'A last kiss for the baby'. This sentimental comment was to achieve a genuine pathos as the piles of Italian dead mounted up on the battlefields of the Isonzo.

3 A unit of crack *bérsaglieri* riflemen marches down an Italian street after mobilisation in May 1915.

4 An early photograph intended to display Italy's combined maritime/aviation skills. A flying boat passes over a monitor armed with twin 380mm guns.

5 A rear-view shot of an Italian 75mm Modello 11 field gun being loaded by its crew. The Modello 11 was designed with mountain warfare in mind, so the barrel had a maximum elevation of 65° to allow for high-angle shooting in mountainous terrain. The gun fired a 6.35kg (14lb) shell and possessed an impressive maximum range of 10,250m (11,200yd).

6 Italian troops race to set up the guns on an armoured train running alongside the Adriatic Sea. Italy and Austria-Hungary shared the coastline around the Adriatic and this stretch of water was to become a much fought-over naval battleground. Italy was particularly prone to hit-and-run raids on her coastline, and armoured trains provided a mobile means of defence where the railway ran by the sea. Despite being essentially a land power Austria-Hungary maintained a small fleet at her Adriatic port of Pola, and in 1914 this included 16 battleships, 18 destroyers, 85 torpedo-boats and 11 submarines.

Battle for the mountains
Italy's Alpine war

1 The old military maxim of 'he who holds the heights holds the valleys' has been fully absorbed by these Italian gunners, who are engaged in raising a 75mm field gun literally up the side of a mountain.

2 Clearly visible against the snow, an Austrian machine-gun team prepares for action. The Schwarzlose machine gun was no lightweight, but was reliable and generally popular with the troops. While the major battles of the war were fought on Italy's eastern border, along the Isonzo River, a bitter struggle was fought for control of the mountain ridges.

3 Some of the extraordinary problems of transportation in the Alps are revealed in this photograph of a wounded man being evacuated to a field hospital.

4 To provide their men with a degree of protection against enemy artillery fire, Austrian mountain troops have cut carefully zig-zagged snow trenches along an important mountain slope.

5 Italian artillerymen drag gun parts and ammunition up a particularly steep slope, eventually to a height of 3400m (10,200ft). The mountain troops used by both Italy and Austria were of a generally superior quality; the very nature of this warfare demanded special skills and powers of endurance.

6 An Italian soldier of an *Alpini* regiment slides down the mountainside on a simple cable device. The *Alpini* were regarded as the elite troops of the Italian Army and fought well in the battle for Trentino in 1916. This soldier is armed with a 6.5mm Mannlicher-Carcano rifle.

7 Tucked away in a snow hole high up on the mountainside, an Austrian sentry watches over the valley below.

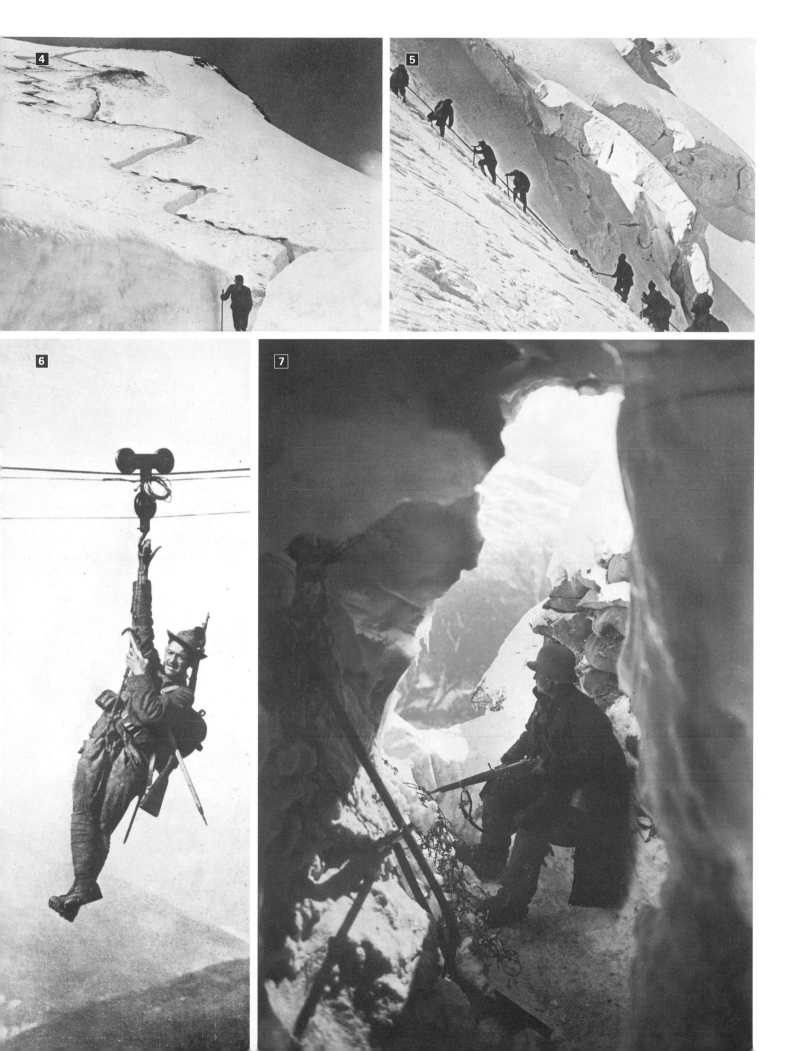

Chapter 4 **The widening war**

World War I began as a European war, but was soon to spread across the globe. New theatres of war emerged while countries far from Europe found themselves inexorably sucked into the great conflict. This was a direct consequence of Europe's acquisition of colonial empires; it was inevitable that these territories should either supply aid to the 'mother' country or find themselves becoming far-flung battlegrounds. As Britain's naval supremacy was virtually worldwide in 1914, Germany had little hope of reinforcing and supplying her scattered colonial possessions, and little was expected of them. It was therefore just a matter of time before the German Empire overseas fell to the Allies, unless Germany won the war in Europe.

In the Pacific, Germany controlled two groups of islands, German New Guinea and Western Samoa, and both were captured by Australian and New Zealand expeditions within a few weeks of the outbreak of war. In China, Germany leased the enclave around the port of Tsingtao, but the Japanese had their own designs on this territory. Shortly after the start of hostilities in Europe, Japan declared war on Germany (23 August) and her forces besieged Tsingtao. Joined by a small British expeditionary force, the Japanese pressed home a major assault against the German fortifications early in November, and forced a German surrender on the 7th.

Africa, however, had been the main victim of German colonial activity, and by 1914 four territories lay under German rule: Togo, the Cameroons, German South-West Africa and German East Africa. On 26 August Togo fell to a Franco-British invasion. The campaign in the Cameroons was distinguished by stiff German resistance, but the administrative centre and Duala wireless station were captured at the end of 1914. German South-West Africa presented greater problems, not least because many of the Afrikaners of South Africa wished to reverse the decision of the Boer War. Outright rebellion broke out in South Africa during September 1914, but although the rebels mustered some 11,000 men, their leadership was divided, and after some initial successes the revolt fizzled out in February 1915. The South Afri-

cans, under the command of the famous Boer general Louis Botha (by this time prime minister of the Union), could only then get to grips with the Germans in South-West Africa. Enemy strongpoints were encircled, and Windhoek, the capital, fell on 12 May. On 9 July General Botha accepted the German surrender.

In German East Africa, the Allies faced a most formidable opponent. Colonel Paul von Lettow-Vorbeck, commanding a small force (never exceeding 15,000 men and consisting chiefly of African askaris), repulsed all efforts at an invasion of the colony until February 1916, when superiority of Allied numbers forced the Germans onto the defensive. Far from beaten, however, von Lettow-Vorbeck converted his army into an irregular force and for the remainder of the war waged a brilliant guerrilla campaign. It was only the news of the armistice in Europe that led him to surrender – on 23 November 1918. This achievement is made all the more notable by the fact that von Lettow-Vorbeck kept busy no fewer than 372,950 troops of the British Empire – British, South African, Rhodesian, Indian and African.

Despite the numbers of troops involved, the capture of Germany's colonies had little strategic significance. Turkey's entry into the war on the side of the Central Powers in November 1914 was a different matter, however. Already Turkey was heavily dependent on German economic and military aid, and her nationalistic ruling party (the 'Young Turks') cherished ambitious territorial designs against the old enemy Russia. Germany was quick to appreciate the advantages of drawing her into the war. The Turkish Empire stretched across the Middle East, and was not only a barrier to Allied reinforcement of Russia through the Black Sea, but also a threat to the Suez Canal and Britain's imperial lifelines. The Turks, enraged by British seizure of ships built for them in British shipyards, were ready enough. Turkish fears of British naval might were overcome when the German battlecruiser *Goeben* and the cruiser *Breslau* sailed through the Dardanelles Straits on 10 August; the two vessels were incorporated into the Turkish Navy, crews included. On 29 October, a Turkish fleet which included these two ships

Below right: Leading light in the 'Young Turks' movement, Enver Pasha pushed Turkey towards war on the side of the Central Powers.

Below centre: General Louis Botha commanded the Allied forces in the reduction of German South-West Africa.

Below: The brilliant guerrilla commander Colonel Paul von Lettow-Vorbeck; he remained unbeaten in the field and only surrendered after news reached him of the armistice in Europe.

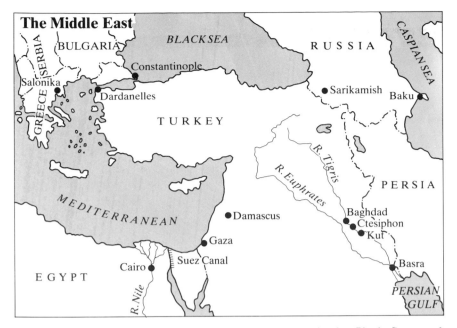

The Middle East

Above: Turkish possessions threatened British interests in the Middle East. Large numbers of British and Empire troops were dispatched to fight the Turks in Mesopotamia, in the defence of Suez, and at Gallipoli. This represented a serious drain of resources away from the main centre of conflict on the Western Front.

bombarded Russian ports in the Black Sea; on 1 November Russia declared war on Turkey, joined four days later by France and Britain.

Turkey's first military act was a long-planned expedition into the Russian Caucasus threatening the Baku oilfields. Under the command of Turkey's leader, Enver Pasha, the assault was launched on 22 December 1914. The Turkish Army was unprepared for the harsh conditions of a Caucasian winter, however, and on 1 January 1915 was severely defeated by the Russians at Sarikamish, in a four-day battle which left only 18,000 Turkish survivors from an original force of 95,000 men. This marked the end of the Turkish offensive against Russia, although fighting continued in a desultory fashion over the next two years. In 1915 the Turks made a number of raids against the Suez Canal from Palestine but these were easily repelled by the defending British and Empire troops.

Turkey's entry into the war seemed to offer an opportunity for sea power – in particular British naval supremacy – to supply the desired alternative to the trench deadlock on the Western Front. British thinking hardened steadily upon an expedition to the Dardanelles, aimed at gaining control of Constantinople and the Bosporus. The goal was to open an ice-free route to Russia through which she could export her grain surplus and import much-needed munitions. It was at first believed that the Royal Navy could carry out such a project without army support. Heavy losses of old French and British battleships to Turkish mines in the Narrows, however, prompted the call for a military expedition also.

The problem was to find the men; by late April a mixed force of British regulars, a naval division, ANZACs (the Australian and New Zealand Army Corps) and French troops was assembled in Egypt under General Sir Ian Hamilton to attack the Dardanelles and occupy the Gallipoli Peninsula. With Canadians heavily engaged at Ypres, and South Africans in South-West Africa, the participation of the Australians and New Zealanders at Gallipoli confirmed the unique contribution of the British self-governing Dominions to the war.

The men went ashore on 25 April, but faced with determined Turkish opposition, and lacking any special equipment for amphibious operations, the

Allies were only able, at heavy cost, to secure tenuous footholds at Cape Helles and Anzac Cove. Turkish counter-attacks nevertheless failed to dislodge the Allies, so that a trench-warfare stalemate similar to that of the Western Front again resulted, made almost unbearable for the troops on the ground by extreme climatic conditions, disease, and critical shortages of supplies and ammunition. In August further landings were made at Suvla Bay, but command failures and inexperience prevented any exploitation from the beach-head. The inability to make any headway on Gallipoli, despite the most desperate attempts by British, French and Anzac troops, and the heavy losses incurred, now led to demands for the abandonment of the campaign. During December and January skilfully conducted evacuations of the beach-head were carried out, marking a sad end to a brave endeavour. The forces of the British Empire suffered a total of 213,980 casualties (114,649 in battle), the French 47,000 and the Turks at least 251,000, although some estimates place this figure at nearer 350,000.

The 1915 British campaign in Mesopotamia began as a simple operation to safeguard oil installations in the Persian Gulf, but the weakness of Turkish resistance along the River Tigris encouraged an advance further inland. A water-borne expedition was dispatched up the Tigris in May, commanded by the ambitious Major-General Charles Townshend. Progress was slow due rather to logistical problems than the Turkish defences. Kut-al-Amara was taken on 28 September 1915 and Townshend prepared for an advance on Baghdad. However, at Ctesiphon on 21 November the Turks repulsed the British column, which fell back on Kut, only to be besieged by a reinforced Turkish Army. Attempts to relieve the British in Kut were unsuccessful; on the point of starvation, the remnants of Townshend's force surrendered on 29 April 1916, a second defeat for Britain at the hands of the Turks.

Turkey, although a secondary enemy, had proved a far tougher opponent than the British had anticipated, and the campaigns in the Middle East were a significant drain on British resources. In the course of the war some 2,500,000 British and Empire troops were sucked into the Middle East conflict, yet none of these campaigns was to have any serious effect on the main war against Germany. Perhaps worst of all was the palpable failure of sea power to resolve the strategic *impasse*, which committed Britain to making her main effort as a land power.

Nor did the Allied expedition at Salonika cause the Germans serious embarrassment. In December 1915 an offensive was launched to strike northward against Bulgaria, but this came to nothing, and the Allied troops fell back to Salonika. Reinforced by the refugee Serbs, now reorganised and re-equipped, and with Italians and contingents from Gallipoli, the force at Salonika grew to a strength of over 600,000 men by 1917. German observers of this great diversion of Allied strength sardonically described Salonika as the 'greatest Allied internment camp' of the war. It was a conspicuous example of the Allied tendency towards dispersal of effort, contrasting sharply with Germany's economical use of small military contingents in support of her allies. Small teams of advisers were dispatched to key areas where their experience could be used to the best effect without being a drain on German resources on the Western Front. This judicious distribution of German weapons, munitions, personnel, and economic aid helped to keep her weakening partners in the field.

Britain calls upon Empire

1 South African mounted troops patrol along the Orange River, frontier between South Africa and the German colony of South-West Africa. In South Africa Britain's call for help against Germany led to virtual civil war when thousands of Boer farmers took up arms against the British, their former enemies during the Boer War. The revolt was crushed, however, and by 9 July 1915 the German colony of South-West Africa was in British hands.

2 Indian troops train with the French Hotchkiss light machine gun on the Western Front. The Indian Army was a volunteer force and despite India's remoteness from the source of the conflict, 1,440,437 men were recruited. The Indians were the first troops from the Empire and Dominions to arrive on the Western Front (23 October 1914).

3 Australia and New Zealand were responsible for the occupation of Germany's Pacific Island colonies. On Nauru, Europeans and natives gather to raise the Union Jack for the first time, 7 November 1914.

4 Canadian armourers in the process of maintaining their Canadian-built .303 Ross rifles. The Ross was found to lack the robustness and reliability needed for a service rifle on the Western Front and was subsequently replaced by the SMLE, although its superior accuracy gave it a lease of life as a sniper's rifle. The first Canadian forces arrived in Britain in October 1914; they achieved divisional status in February 1915, and by 1917 had become an army corps of four divisions. Altogether Canada raised 628,964 men for the Allied cause.

5 Wearing their traditional slouch hats, jovial Australian troops march towards the front line near Amiens, September 1916. The ANZAC forces gained a fighting reputation at Gallipoli and later on the Western Front. The New Zealanders fielded their own division and there were enough Australian volunteers to form a corps of five divisions. By mid-1917 the three Dominions had ten first-class divisions on the Western Front and these formations became increasingly important as the offensive vanguard of the British Army in France and Belgium.

6 Pioneers from an Indian regiment wait to embark for East Africa. After 1915 the bulk of the Indian Army was stationed in the east, deployed in several theatres of war strung out across half the globe. Besides helping guard British trade and communications east of the Suez Canal, the Indian Army played a key role in the defeat of Turkey. One of the major achievements of World War I was the commitment of the Empire and Dominions to the war against the Central Powers; 2,950,051 was their total manpower contribution, as against 5,704,416 from Britain.

Turkey at war

1 The German influence upon the Turkish Army extended to its artillery. Here a Krupps 7.7cm field gun bombards Allied troops at Gallipoli.

2 Headgear apart, these Turkish soldiers conform to the Western models insisted upon by Enver Pasha as he attempted to drag Turkey into the modern world.

3 Brandishing an Islamic standard, Turkish troops cheerfully set out for war.

4 A view across the Golden Horn in 1914. Lying at anchor is the German cruiser *Breslau*, whose arrival with the *Goeben* effectively pushed Turkey into war on the side of the Central Powers.

5 A German adviser (centre, with woollen fez) poses with Turkish staff officers for a group photograph.

6 Dead children lie abandoned, tragic victims of Turkey's virtual genocidal policy against the Armenian minority. Once war had broken out the Christian Armenians were seen as being in league with the Russians. On 11 June 1915 the Turkish government decided to deport them, and during this process atrocities took place on a massive scale.

7 German aid to Turkey took the form of providing advisers to train the Turks in the art of modern warfare plus a few key items of military hardware. The vast empty spaces that comprised the Ottoman Empire made the aircraft an invaluable reconnaissance tool. This aircraft has been transported to Turkey along the famous Berlin to Baghdad railway and is now being unloaded for reassembly. For a limited outlay, Germany thus gave Turkey the power to tie down hundreds of thousands of Allied soldiers.

Gallipoli
Amphibious assault

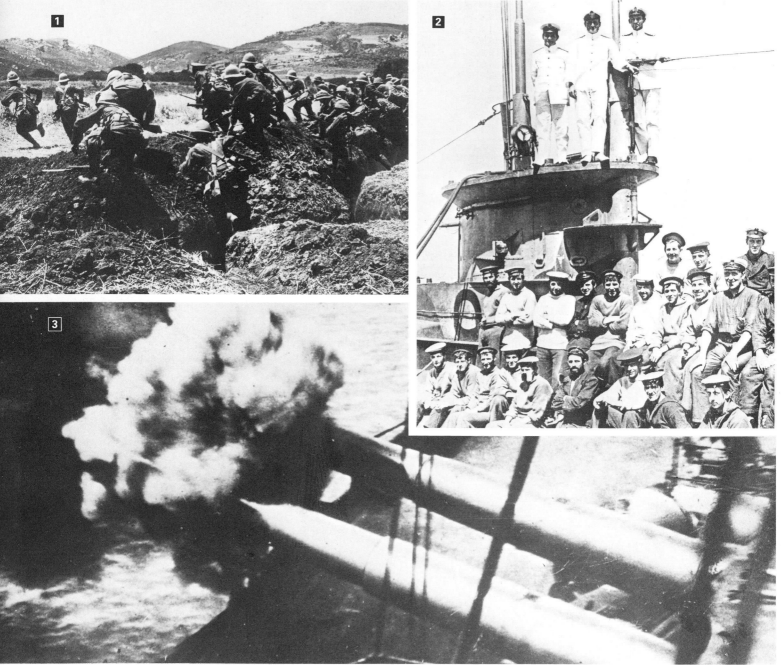

1 The Dardanelles campaign had begun as a purely naval venture but the ships' failure to force a passage through the straits led to calls for amphibious landings. In preparation for this, men of the 2nd Royal Naval Brigade practise an attack across no man's land.

2 The crew of *E-11*, following the submarine's successful return from sinking Turkish ships in the Bosporus.

3 The twin 15in guns of HMS *Queen Elizabeth* fire on the Turkish shore batteries at Gallipoli, 18 March 1915. Forced to operate close-in, the British warships were vulnerable to underwater mines and submarine attack, and several vessels were lost.

4 The obsolete British battleship HMS *Majestic* begins to list as she sinks off Gallipoli on 27 May, victim of an attack by the submarine *U-51*.

5 A shell lands near SS *River Clyde*, an old collier converted to carry the 2000 men who formed the first assault wave on 'V' Beach. Despite attempts to get the men from ship to shore with the utmost speed, hundreds were cut down by Turkish machine-gun and rifle fire.

6 A Turkish officer directs a machine-gun crew on 25 April 1915, the date of the first Allied landings. Their positions overlooking the landing beaches gave the Turks a huge advantage.

7 Men of the Lancashire Fusiliers are crammed into a landing vessel, en route for the beaches. This regiment distinguished itself in the initial landings on 25 April by securing 'W' Beach and winning six VCs in the process.

Gallipoli
Trench stalemate

1 The French Army sent a considerable force to the Dardanelles, to fight alongside the British and ANZAC contingents. This Frenchman, armed with an 8mm Berthier mle 1892 carbine, peers cautiously over the top of a communication trench.

2 Australian troops and men of the Royal Naval Division share a crowded forward trench. The soldier on the left examines Turkish positions through his trench periscope, while to his right another soldier is setting up a 'sniperscope', a periscope-type device for firing a rifle without exposing the firer's head and upper torso. Accuracy was poor, however.

3 The view from Plugg's Plateau looking down on one of the more sheltered bays of the Gallipoli Peninsula, with its loading pier, hospital tents and stocks of equipment.

4 One of the few guns of reasonable calibre available to the British during the Dardanelles campaign – a 60-pounder at maximum recoil. The lack of suitable guns was compounded by equally serious shortages of ammunition.

5 British troops 'go over the top' in a fruitless attempt to drive the Turks off the Gallipoli Peninsula. The Turks were too well entrenched, and the Allies lacked sufficient heavy weapons to shift them.

6 An Australian 'digger' gives a wounded Turk a drink of precious water. While there was little love lost between the Allies and the Turks, the harshness of the environment forged a bond of shared hardship. Thus, for example, at the end of an engagement a truce would often be called for the collection of the dead and wounded in no man's land.

Mesopotamia
British humiliation at Kut

1 The SS *Julnar* embarks with its complement of troops, supplies and weapons (two 18-pounders forward). This flat-bottomed river boat was part of General Townshend's column, nicknamed 'Townshend's Regatta'.

2 Beyond Kut Turkish resistance began to increase and Townshend's column was repulsed at Ctesiphon, a desert settlement dominated by the great Roman arch. The ordinary British soldier had little interest in the glories of antiquity, as this contemporary doggerel suggests: 'Some calls it Ctesiphon, some calls it Cestiphon, but I calls it Pistupon.'

3 Townshend (centre with cap) and his staff at Kut. After falling back to Kut the British force was surrounded and in December 1915 the Turks began to lay siege.

4 A number of attempts were made to relieve and resupply the British garrison at Kut. A combined expedition of land forces and gunboats tried to batter their way through but determined Turkish resistance frustrated this plan. With its very shallow draught the gunboat *Firefly* was a useful military vessel, armed with 6in guns and capable of carrying heavy loads of weapons, equipment and men.

5 After the attempt to raise the siege had failed, supplies were airlifted into the city. In the camp of 30 Squadron a BE2c aircraft is loaded with food for the garrison, which by the spring of 1916 was slowly beginning to starve.

6 Led by British officers, a squadron of Indian cavalry advances towards Kut. The campaign in Mesopotamia was an Indian Army operation, and an increasing number of Indians were sent there.

7 Indian troops captured at Kut photographed immediately after an exchange of prisoners. The Turks adopted a callous attitude towards their captives and these cases of severe malnutrition were not uncommon. The beleaguered garrison at Kut had finally surrendered to the Turks on 29 April 1916. The fall of Kut was perhaps the most humiliating defeat suffered by Britain during the entire war.

German East Africa

1 A British soldier explains the techniques of machine-gun fire to native troops in East Africa. Both sides made great use of native forces in the long-drawn-out East African campaign.

2 The British monitor HMS *Severn* tows a seaplane up the Rufigi River in German East Africa. Once the German troops under von Lettow-Vorbeck had gone over to fighting a guerrilla campaign, the British were faced with the problem of tracking down an elusive enemy operating in millions of square miles of bush and jungle. Aircraft were in short supply but were a vital means of rapidly surveying large areas.

3 A motley collection of German askaris parades for the camera. They are armed with the 1888 model Mauser, and their equipment is the old M1887/89 leather pattern. Denied access to replacements, the uniforms of the German askaris deteriorated steadily as the war progressed. Their somewhat bizarre appearance is accentuated by their own native headgear.

4 The guard of the 1/4th King's African Rifles compares favourably with the askaris, each man being fully kitted out with a uniform, adequate footwear, a rifle, and leather ammunition pouches.

5 Light field guns of the German Army in East Africa create clouds of smoke as they fire a salvo towards enemy positions. These old guns used a gunpowder-based propellant.

6 A carefully prepared photograph of a *Schutztruppe* (colonial troops) workshop in German East Africa. Workmen hammer out a forging, possibly for the repair of the aircraft at the back of the workshop. The need for mechanical improvisation increased as von Lettow-Vorbeck's small forces became more and more hard-pressed. An extraordinary attempt was made to supply von Lettow-Vorbeck with a Zeppelin from Germany in November 1917, but over the Sudan it turned back, under the mistaken impression that the Germans were about to surrender.

Chapter 5

Verdun and the Somme

Throughout 1915 the Central Powers had one great strategic advantage, the ability to wage war on interior lines, and they put it to good use. Their strategic railways enabled them to transfer forces swiftly from front to front. The Allies had no such facility; thus, while the Germans could move 24 divisions from west to east in a month, it took four months to transport nine divisions from France to Egypt or *vice versa*. In the face of this overwhelming difficulty, under Joffre's guidance, the Allies were slowly working towards a strategy of simultaneous offensives against the Central Powers. The Inter-Allied Military Conference at Chantilly, held in December 1915, formulated the Allies' broad strategic plan for 1916: concentric military, naval and economic pressure to crush Germany and her confederates, of which the central feature would be a decisive French attack with strong British support.

In February 1916, however, Germany herself passed to the offensive in the west; General von Falkenhayn planned a mortal blow against the French Army, weakened by almost 2,000,000 casualties since the war began. This time, the usual hope of a breakthrough was exchanged for the prospect of 'bleeding France to death' by attacking a particular sector of the French line which they would feel compelled to defend, regardless of loss. This was the true beginning of undisguised attritional warfare.

The salient around the fortress of Verdun was chosen as the killing-ground; not only was it of strong emotional value to the French, it also allowed the Germans to bring the maximum amount of heavy artillery to bear on the defenders. Artillery was the cornerstone of the tactical plan: limited assaults by the infantry would seize key points in order to draw in French reserves for grinding in the 'mill' of the German guns.

The German Fifth Army, under the command of the Kaiser's son, Crown Prince Wilhelm, was to attack Verdun: six infantry divisions (with three in reserve), on a front of 12km (8 miles), supported by an array of more than 1200 artillery pieces, nearly half of which were of heavy calibre. This array was concealed behind the front line with utmost secrecy. Reports of a German build-up were discounted by the French High Command, who regarded Verdun as a quiet sector, and had stripped its forts of heavy artillery to supply the active armies.

Just after 0700 hours on 21 February 1916 the Germans opened their bombardment of French positions, the most devastating yet experienced in warfare. In the afternoon of the 21st groups of German infantry advanced into the shattered French front-line trenches. Over the next few days the Germans advanced steadily, a notable success being the capture of Fort Douaumont on 25 February.

It was at this stage that General Philippe Pétain arrived as commander of the Second Army defending Verdun. An excellent tactician, Pétain had gained a reputation as a general who cared for his men. He immediately set about organising the supply, reinforcement and relief of his hard-pressed troops. The road from Bar-le-Duc was the only route into Verdun

not under German artillery fire – this vital artery was called *La Voie Sacrée* ('the sacred way') – and along it 3000 lorries a day transported the men, weapons, ammunition and stores that kept Verdun alive.

The German commanders were surprised by the tenacity of the French defence as their own casualties mounted in the face of the Second Army's increasing artillery fire and skilfully mounted counter-attacks. Throughout March, April and May the battle raged with undiminished intensity – if the French were being put through the mill then so too were the Germans. Yet the attackers continued to gain deceptive successes: Fort de Vaux fell on 7 June and Pétain made plans for an evacuation to the east bank of the Meuse. But on 1 July the long-awaited Allied offensive on the Somme opened; German reinforcements were re-routed away from Verdun and on the 11th von Falkenhayn closed down the offensive.

From the end of July, the French went over to the offensive, and in a series of ferocious counter-attacks regained much of the ground lost in the early stages of the battle. On 18 December a final and highly successful French assault signalled the end of the struggle for Verdun, a contest which lasted ten months and which cost the French 362,000 men against a German figure of 336,000. The French had held Verdun; the army was battered but intact; von Falkenhayn's plan had failed and he himself was dismissed on 27 August, to be replaced by the successful team of von Hindenburg and Ludendorff.

All through the first half of 1916, there were French demands for General Haig to commit his forces in order to relieve the German pressure on Verdun. Although the numbers of the BEF were rising steadily (36 divisions in December 1915, 58 by June 1916), Haig knew that they were insufficiently trained and equipped, and so fought to prevent their being frittered away before the great summer offensive. His army was the visible product of an economic and social revolution in Britain. Whole new industries were created to meet the unprecedented demand for materials of war. Millions of men were removed from civilian life, while demands for manpower in industry constantly grew; in consequence, for the first time large numbers of women took jobs previously exclusive to men and began to make a major contribution to the wartime economy.

The character of the great Allied 1916 offensive drastically changed as the Battle of Verdun wore on. Originally conceived as a massive French attack with substantial British backing, by June it had become apparent that the British would have to take the leading role. The location of the offensive, decided by General Joffre, remained, however, unchanged – the junction of the two armies just north of the River Somme.

The main attack was to be made by the recently formed British Fourth Army under General Sir Henry Rawlinson. Eleven divisions were deployed for the first assault, supported by five French south of the Somme. The British relied heavily on their enormously expanded artillery and lavish ammunition supplies; Rawlinson had 2029 guns and howitzers for his 23km

Below: General Philippe Pétain, the saviour of Verdun. Appointed to command the French Second Army, he raised the morale of his troops by being seen to care for their needs. The defence of Verdun was an epic of its kind, vast casualties being inflicted on both sides. Although the city was threatened in June, the French managed to hang on, and through a series of counter-offensives in the second half of 1916 regained most of the ground lost at the beginning of the battle.

Above: General Sir Douglas Haig (left) makes a point to his Prime Minister, David Lloyd George, while Joffre (centre) looks on. Haig replaced French as Commander-in-Chief of British forces on the Western Front in December 1915.

Below. On the Western Front 1916 was dominated by two battles: Verdun and the Somme.

(14-mile) frontage, and they fired off no fewer than 1,732,873 rounds during their eight-day preliminary bombardment. However, of this total of guns, only 452 were heavies (compared with 700 on the French front, which was only half as wide), and some 30 per cent of the ammunition supplied by the new industries was to prove defective. Nor was the strength of the German positions, with shelters dug deep into the chalk downs of Picardy, appreciated until these were captured – at high cost.

Confident that the artillery had crushed the defence, the British infantry went 'over the top' in perfect order at 0730 on 1 July, only to be cut down in waves. A total of 57,470 officers and men became casualties on that day, about 20,000 being killed outright. Only on the right, alongside the French, did they achieve any success; elsewhere the assault was stopped in its tracks, mostly without even reaching the German positions. The French themselves, whose attack took the Germans by surprise, and was supported by plentiful artillery, made considerable gains at relatively small cost. The contrast between their flexible infantry tactics and the straight rigid lines of the British advance – offering wonderful targets for artillery and machine guns – has prompted many to blame British tactics for the heavy loss. The chief reason, however, was the failure of the artillery to overwhelm the defenders. The British had more guns than ever before but still not enough; and they would require even larger mountains of ammunition – preferably without defects.

The first of July 1916 was a freak occasion in the war; never again did the British suffer losses on that scale; and never again during the Battle of the Somme did the French prove so successful. There was no question of not continuing the offensive – the first day of the Somme was the 132nd day of the Battle of Verdun, and it would have been unthinkable for the British to stop fighting after only one day (even if the Germans had permitted it). The German response was, in any case,

These orders account for the 330 German attacks or counter-attacks punctuating the Allied advances.

Yet the advances continued steadily. A dawn attack on 14 July showed what the Kitchener Armies were capable of, and indicated considerable improvements in British staff work; its success surprised both the Germans and the more unimaginative British regular officers. Yet every success turned into trench-warfare slogging as the counter-attacks came in. On 15 September came a historic occasion: the first use of tanks in battle – a British innovation. The few MkI tanks available were no war-winners, but their successors were to make a significant contribution in the future. More important was the fact that, for the *only* time in the war, the Allies managed to strike simultaneous blows: a final offensive by the Russians in the east, the Romanian entry into the war, an Italian offensive and both British and French also attacking. The Central Powers were badly shaken, but held on.

The final act of the battle was the capture of Beaumont-Hamel, on 13 November. Already the battle area was turning into a sea of mud, and the snows and frost of the war's worst winter were beginning. So the great offensive ended, in disappointment and heavy loss for all. British casualties during the 142 days of the Somme amounted to 415,000; the French, even in a secondary role, lost over 200,000; German losses were so great that they deliberately disguised them – they probably equalled those of the British and French together. Taken in conjunction with their losses at Verdun, and their losses in repelling the very powerful Russian offensives of the year, the conclusion is that the old peace-trained German Army had now disappeared. The Somme, the Germans later admitted, was 'the muddy grave of the German field army'. The British, on the other hand, had now attained professional status, and with only two short intermissions it would be the BEF that henceforth engaged the main body of the German Army in battle until it was defeated.

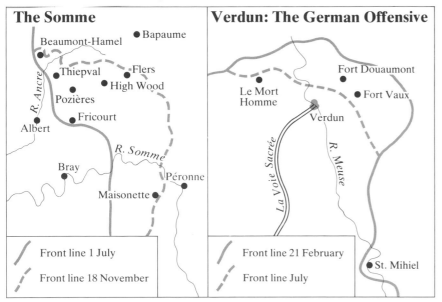

The Somme

Bapaume
Beaumont-Hamel
Thiepval — Flers
High Wood
Pozières
Fricourt
Albert
R. Ancre
R. Somme
Bray
Péronne
Maisonette

/ Front line 1 July

/ Front line 18 November

Verdun: The German Offensive

Fort Douaumont
Le Mort Homme
Fort Vaux
Verdun
La Voie Sacrée
R. Meuse

/ Front line 21 February

/ Front line July

St. Mihiel

Far right: Lieutenant-General Sir Henry Rawlinson outside his headquarters, July 1916. As commander of the British Fourth Army his troops opened the offensive on the Somme, suffering nearly 60,000 casualties on 1 July.

extremely vigorous, giving the battle the savage quality which it retained to the end. General von Below, commanding their Second Army, told his men on 3 July: 'The important ground lost in certain places will be recaptured ... the important thing is to hold our present positions at any cost.... The enemy should have to carve his way over heaps of corpses.'

Verdun
The German mincer

1 A section of German infantry just out of the line at Verdun. The fresh-faced enthusiasm of 1914 is gone forever; these men are the tired veterans of trench warfare. Like front-line soldiers of every conflict of the modern age, these troops carry extra ammunition, in bandoliers slung around their necks.

2 'Big Bertha' in action. The massive 42cm M-Gerat siege howitzer hurls its 810kg (1790lb) shell towards French fortifications around Verdun. Maximum range was 9300m (10,200yd) and both conventional high-explosive and special armour-piercing projectiles were used at Verdun. This was the first great artillery battle: 2,500,000 shells supported the opening assault, and after four months of battle a total of 24,000,000 had been expended.

3 German infantry pass by their own barbed-wire *chevaux de frise* before descending into the valley and then on to the French positions in the distance.

4 Crouching in a forward trench a German assault party waits impatiently for the order to attack. The scale of the artillery bombardments had convinced the German commanders that their infantry would be merely called upon to take physical possession of the battered enemy trenches. To the Germans' consternation pockets of French troops invariably survived the German guns, and by breaking the cohesion of the German attack, managed to prevent any breakthrough.

5 The outline of Fort de Vaux can be picked out in this aerial photograph of the shell-pocked landscape around Verdun. The fortress fell to the Germans on 7 June 1916.

6 The awe-inspiring sight of a land-mine going up in no man's land.

7 An assault team of German infantrymen experiments with a portable flamethrower. First used at Verdun on 21 February, these weapons caused an initial outcry. But more frightening than effective, experienced troops had little to fear from them. Slow-moving, conspicuous and highly vulnerable, the German flamethrower teams were choice targets for French snipers and so they became increasingly more cautious as the battle progressed.

Verdun
Defence and counter-attack

1 Heads down, French troops advance across no man's land. The German offensive against Verdun petered out in July 1916, allowing the battered French defenders some respite from a battle that had been going on for five months. In October and November the French began their counter-offensive, which regained them nearly all the ground they had previously lost.

2 *La Voie Sacrée*: the lifeline that kept Verdun supplied with men and munitions. A convoy of trucks stretches to the horizon. Sufficient numbers of troops to form a division were employed solely to keep the road from Bar-le-Duc to Verdun open and the trucks running.

3 Like ants, German reinforcements slowly wind their way along a communication trench to the front line. The aerial photograph gives some idea of the appalling conditions encountered at Verdun.

4 An enormous 40cm Modèle 15 howitzer is prepared for firing. The Modèle 15 was capable of throwing a 900kg (2000lb) shell out to a maximum range of 15,000m (16,400yd). Two of these railway howitzers were used to smash through the carapace of Fort Douaumont prior to its recapture by the French on 24 October 1916.

5 A Hotchkiss mle 1914 machine gun, shown here in an anti-aircraft role. The mle 1914 was an air-cooled weapon – hence the 'doughnut' cooling rings around the barrel – in contrast to the water-cooled machine guns of the other combatant armies. The gun was fed by a series of 24-round strips which prevented the sustained fire possible with the standard belt-fed system. Attempts were made to remedy this by adapting the strips into a 3-round link belt.

6 A famous photograph of French troops resting in a dug-out at Verdun. Implicit in the German Chief of Staff's planning for Verdun was the mistaken belief that the French Army would lack cohesion and morale during a long battle. The ordinary soldiers of the French Army proved this to be untrue, as they stoically withstood the pressure on them. Casualties for both sides were at least 700,000 men, the French suffering slightly more and the Germans correspondingly less than half of the total.

Battle of the Somme – Day 1

1 A British 9.2in gun fires in support of infantry operations, 1 July 1916. For the first time the artillery had been able to build up a good stock of ammunition, so that 1,732,873 rounds were fired in the eight-day bombardment which preceded the assault. However about a third of these were 'duds', and there were too few large calibres to be effective.

2 A line of British infantry goes over the top and advances in good order towards its target of La Boisselle on the morning of 1 July. Here the Germans were well-prepared for the British attack and their machine guns cut them down in swathes.

3 A mountain of empty shell cases near Fricourt. The numbers of heavy guns available to the British increased significantly as the battle developed, and this and other improvements gave the artillery a new importance. Throughout the entire course of the Battle of the Somme, British artillery fired over 27,000,000 rounds.

4 A mine explodes under the Hawthorn Redoubt just ten minutes before the assault on Beaumont-Hamel.

5 Under heavy fire British troops can be seen pushing forward to German trenches near Mametz. The Germans were amazed at the ponderous good order of the British advance which made them perfect targets.

6 British infantrymen clamber over their own wire before attempting to cross no man's land. Those who made it over to the German trenches found the German wire largely intact.

7 A British soldier carries in a wounded comrade from the 1st Bedfords, at Beaumont-Hamel. In the one day of fighting the British Army suffered 57,470 casualties, by far the highest in its entire history.

Battle of the Somme
The struggle continues

1 A dead German soldier lies outside his dug-out, a victim of the final British assault on Beaumont-Hamel, November 1916.

2 A battery of 9.2in howitzers of the Royal Australian Artillery firing on German positions near Fricourt in August 1916.

3 German troops run forward to reinforce front-line positions. Von Falkenhayn and his army commander on the Somme, von Below, issued orders that no ground was to be surrendered to the Allies, and that any ground lost was to be regained without delay. It has been estimated that von Below's Second Army launched 330 distinct attacks and counter-attacks against the British and French on the Somme. The constant assaults brought about the vast casualty rates that made the Somme the bloodiest battle in history – a rough estimate was 600,000 killed and wounded for the British and French, and a similar figure for the Germans.

4 Men of the 1st Battalion, Lancashire Fusiliers fix bayonets in a communication trench.

5 Battle-weary British soldiers cluster around a knocked-out tank after the capture of Flers. The Battle of Flers-Courcelette on 15 September marked the introduction of the tank in battle, and although many of the Mk1s broke down, the few that reached the German lines easily flattened the barbed wire.

6 The Somme, November 1916. The battle came to an end as torrential rain turned the battlefield into a vast quagmire and near-Arctic weather heralded the coldest winter for over 30 years. The Battle of the Somme had been the first major offensive to be conducted by the British Army, and despite massive casualty lists it had proved itself a match for its German opponent.

Britain's home front

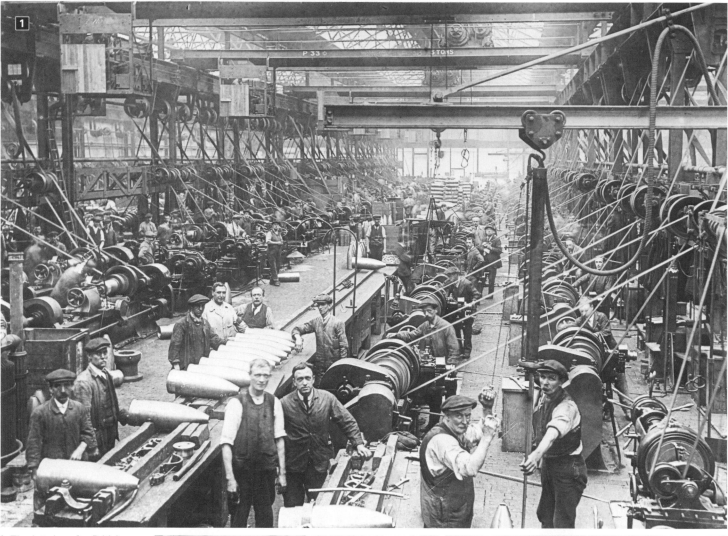

1 The interior of a British munitions factory. Of all the major combatants Britain was the least prepared to wage a modern continental war. New industries and business methods had to be developed to meet the ever-increasing demand for weapons and equipment. The supply of munitions remained a problem until the end of 1915, when Lloyd George's presence at the Ministry of Munitions began to take effect. Partly as a quality-control method Lloyd George introduced new licensing laws to regulate the consumption of alcohol.

2 Women workers pack fuze heads in the Coventry Ordnance Works. The war brought large numbers of women into the work-force, giving them an economic freedom previously unthinkable.

3 A female factory worker in the Midlands uses an oxyacetylene torch to weld frame lugs for aircraft. The war created new industries as well as new possibilities for women. Freed from economic dependence on the male breadwinner, women's social status rose and the progress of political emancipation was encouraged.

4 Although in no way comparable to the horrors of trench warfare, the war was literally brought home to the civil population in Britain by the advent of German aerial attacks. Workmen inspect damage to a building in King's Cross, London, caused by a German bombing raid on 17 July 1917.

5 A regular feature of life in London during the gloomy years of wartime: award-giving ceremonies with rows of widows and mothers dressed in black awaiting their next-of-kins' posthumous awards.

6 Conscientious objectors serving prison sentences for refusing to fight. A total of 985 'absolutists' formed the hard core of the movement, although other objectors escaped imprisonment and were given the chance of doing civilian work of 'national importance'. Conscription was introduced in January 1916, imposing service on unmarried men without exemption certificates, and was extended in May 1916 to cover all men between the ages of 18 and 41.

Behind the lines

1 A British soldier scans a price noticeboard at a British-run canteen at Givency in France in 1917. Run by voluntary societies, canteens such as this offered soldiers out of the line a taste of normality, British 'luxuries' at reasonable British prices. The societies and charitable bodies run by Christian organisations were always keen to keep men away from the more dubious French forms of entertainment, the bars and the brothels. However, the British Army accepted the men's need for sex, and organised its own brothel system.

2 A meticulously arranged photograph of French troops relaxing after a spell in the trenches. While the British went to considerable lengths to look after their soldiers away from the front line, the French Army paid little attention to the welfare of its men. Common complaints included poor food, lack of leave and inadequate medical facilities.

3 The British authorities had always emphasised the virtues of sport for keeping their men occupied. Their lead is followed in this boxing match, arranged between a local French champion and an American boxer.

4 When the troops came out of the line efforts were made to clean them up. Most formations would have a delousing facility.

5 Concert parties were a popular feature of life out of the trenches and the Fifth Army's 'Gaieties' played to an invariably packed auditorium.

6 Indian civilians butcher meat for British troops at Arras. As the war progressed menial tasks were increasingly undertaken by gangs of foreign labourers recruited from the Empire.

7 British troops haggle over the price of mistletoe at a Christmas market, 1916.

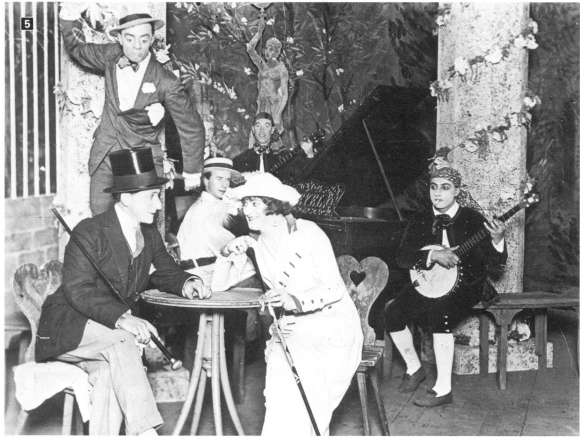

Casualties

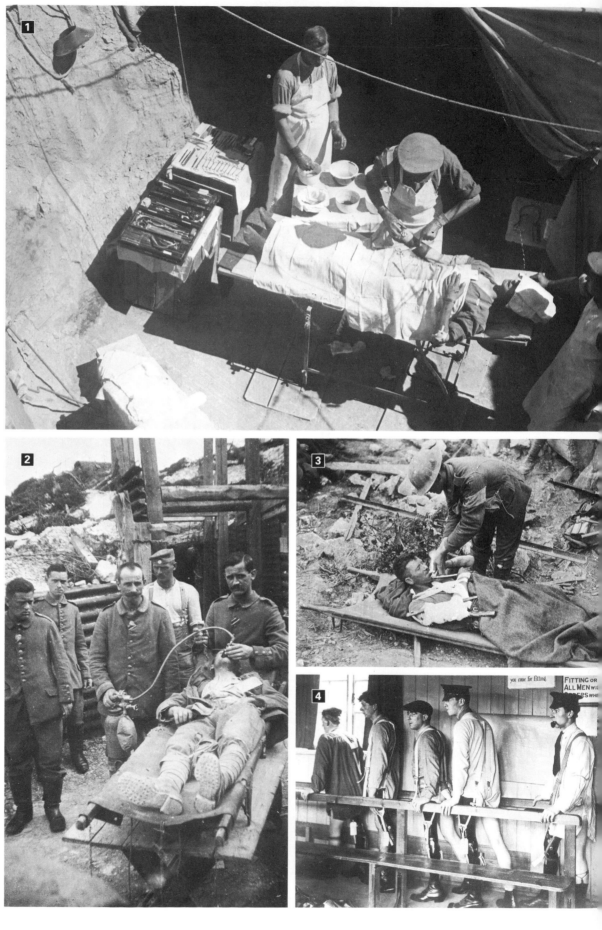

1 World War I was the first conflict to make commonplace the major developments in surgery and hygiene that had occurred during the previous 50 years. Even in remote locations (Palestine in this photograph) and on the edge of the battlefield itself, surgical operations could be performed. This man is having a bullet removed from his arm.

2 Poison gas introduced new types of casualties requiring special treatment. The effect of gas on unprotected men produced horrifying damage to the body (notably to the respiratory system), and although the number of deaths caused by gas was surprisingly low (only two per cent of fatalities were attributed to mustard gas, for example), its psychological effect was enormous.

3 Once a man was wounded he might receive immediate first aid from his mates. A bayonet scabbard and an entrenching tool handle provide an improvised splint for this Canadian, his arm broken by shrapnel. In addition, this soldier has been given a cigarette, a traditional goodwill gesture among men in the trenches.

4 The sheer scale of casualties and the improved chances of surviving a battlefield wound in World War I ensured that there were large numbers of amputees and cripples, with their own special needs and forms of treatment.

5 Wounded troops are prepared for evacuation from a communications trench to a casualty clearing station for further treatment.

6/7 Before the advent of plastic and cosmetic surgery little could be done for men so badly mutilated, except to provide them with masks such as this.

8 Under a portrait of their emperor, wounded Austro-Hungarians are shown recovering in the convalescent ward of a Viennese hospital.

a future which would not be long delayed.

Surface warfare, meanwhile, continued on more familiar lines. It was a blow to British naval prestige when the German ships *Goeben* and *Breslau* escaped unharmed out of the Mediterranean to Constantinople, and precipitated Turkish entry into the war. There were inconclusive forays by light forces of both sides in the North Sea, with a balance of advantage to the British. On the other hand, the German raiding squadrons were able to reach and bombard towns on the east coast of England and escape with impunity; a populace totally unschooled in the character of modern naval war was much dismayed at this. However, improved radio surveillance of German movements was making all such activities more and more hazardous. Both the Hartlepool/Scarborough raid in December 1914 and the Dogger Bank action in January 1915 came close to being disastrous for the Germans. Their unexpected encounters on each occasion with superior British forces instilled in them a great respect for British Naval Intelligence – though they never grasped where they were going wrong. Over a year would pass before the German battle squadrons ventured out into the North Sea again; this was a victory for wireless telegraphy, interception and cryptanalysis.

These secret matters were known to very few; what was obvious to the general public of the world was the progress of surface warfare where it could be observed by neutrals and reported in newspapers. The raiding activities of German light cruisers in distant waters – in particular the *Emden*, under her skilful and chivalrous captain Karl von Muller, in the Indian Ocean – attracted much attention. One by one, however, these were eliminated, radio or radio interception generally playing an important part in their destruction.

The most powerful of Germany's cruiser forces was Vice-Admiral Maximilian von Spee's East Asiatic Squadron in the Pacific; this consisted of the two heavy cruisers, *Scharnhorst* and *Gneisenau*, each with eight 210mm guns, and three light cruisers of the *Emden* type. Against von Spee was arrayed an Australian squadron in the South Seas which included the fast, modern battlecruiser *Australia* with eight 12in guns, capable of destroying the whole German squadron by herself. When Japan entered the war on 23 August she added to the Allied strength two modern battlecruisers able to steam at 27 knots, and four smaller ones. Faced with this, von Spee had little choice; he set course across the Pacific, and on 1 November his crack heavy cruisers sank the two elderly cruisers *Good Hope* and *Monmouth* under Rear-Admiral Sir Christopher Cradock at Cape Coronel.

The British response was swift and devastating. The new First Sea Lord, Admiral Fisher, dispatched two of the battlecruisers he had designed himself, *Invincible* and *Inflexible*, armed like *Australia* with 12in guns, under Vice-Admiral Sir Doveton Sturdee, to the Falkland Islands to bar von Spee's passage into the Atlantic. There, on 8 December, the rival forces met, and after a long running fight all the German vessels except one light cruiser were sent to the bottom. Von Spee died in the action, with both his sons. To the British public, a Nelsonian retribution had been inflicted upon an impertinent enemy; they were unconcerned at the length of time it had taken their great ships to sink their far weaker opponents. Few were disposed to question whether Fisher's battlecruisers were viable naval units or not – nearly a year

and a half would elapse before the answer became apparent.

The greatest surface action of the war, and in terms of numbers of ships, the greatest in history – 259 vessels engaged – came on 31 May 1916. The Germans were once more attempting a familiar tactic: to cripple the Grand Fleet by destroying sections of it in detail. The British response was also familiar: radio surveillance enabled the Grand Fleet to put to sea before the Germans it intended to catch had even left harbour. Yet in the battle that followed, it was a communications breakdown (faulty signals and sheer lack of signals) that robbed the British of victory. Although they surprised the German fleet, they were unable to capitalise on their advantage. Good guns, good ammunition and, above all, good shooting enabled the Germans to inflict heavier damage than they sustained. Three out of nine of Fisher's battlecruisers were sent to the bottom by devastating explosions that tore them apart, killing virtually their entire crews. Good tactics by Admiral von Scheer, the German Commander-in-Chief, then enabled his fleet to escape its numerically superior enemy during the night. Tactically, this battle, known to the British as Jutland and to the Germans as the Skagerrak, was a German success; strategically, it was a British victory – the High Seas Fleet played no further significant part in the war until, in November 1918, its demoralised crews broke into open mutiny.

As the summer of 1916 wore on, with the Eastern Front once more aflame and the Battle of the Somme coming to its climax, Germany's position became desperate. The demand for 'unrestricted U-boat warfare' became more urgent than ever, and was now backed by the Army High Command. By October, the U-boats themselves had effectively settled the matter: a sharp rise in the number of sinkings without warning brought an equally significant rise in the amount of shipping sunk. From October 1916 to October 1917 the monthly world total never fell below 300,000 tonnes. On 1 February 1917, this state of affairs received formal recognition: the 'unrestricted' campaign was declared to have begun, and at once produced alarming results: 548,671 tonnes of shipping were sunk in that month, 603,369 in March, and the devastating record figure of 894,147 tonnes in April.

There was now a very real possibility that the Allies might lose the war, with the cutting-off of overseas supplies on which they (Britain above all) depended. The remainder of the war at sea was, in fact, the war against the U-boats. This was decided partly by method – the revival of the convoy system on which British trade had always depended in war – and partly by technology. Convoys made it increasingly difficult for U-boats to find targets and also to attack them. Technology – depth charges, improved mines, hydrophones, increasing use of aircraft and always the contribution of radio-based Intelligence – steadily overcame the U-boat advantages of invisibility and surprise. In April 1918, for the first time, Allied shipping production exceeded losses; this marked the defeat of the U-boats. By the end of the war, no fewer than 178 of them had been lost, 140 definitely by enemy action. Yet their morale remained high, and as the German Navy collapsed in mutiny and revolution, only the U-boat crews continued to do their duty, despite casualties amounting to about 30 per cent of all who served in the submarine arm. And they had given a very clear pointer to the naval war of the future.

Above: Admiral Sir David Beatty, the commander of the British battlecruisers 1914–16. Involved in the Battles of Dogger Bank and Jutland, his battlecruiser fleets were dogged by signalling problems and inferior gunnery to that of the Germans. He succeeded Jellicoe as Commander-in-Chief of the British Fleet towards the end of 1916.

Below: Admiral Hipper led the German battlecruisers at Jutland. Although outnumbered, his forces inflicted some spectacular reverses on the British, and his conduct in the battle won high praise from all quarters. Hipper was appointed Commander-in-Chief of the German Fleet in August 1918.

The commerce raiders

1 Prisoners wait on deck of the German raider *Möwe* on her return to Kiel on 22 March 1917, after a four-month cruise in which she sank or captured 27 merchant ships.

2 The *Seeadler* in dock, disguised as a Norwegian cargo ship. By 1915–16 the first generation of cruiser-raiders had been identified; their successors were elaborately camouflaged.

3 The forward 6in gun of the British monitor *Severn* is made ready for action against the light cruiser *Königsberg*, June 1915.

4 Local natives stare at the *Königsberg* as she steams up the Rufiji estuary. The *Königsberg* operated in the Indian Ocean where she sank a number of vessels (including HMS *Pegasus* off Zanzibar), but was herself caught and destroyed in the Rufiji Delta in June 1915.

5 The SMS *Dresden* began her raiding career off the coast of Brazil before being called south to join von Spee's squadron. She escaped the disaster of the Falklands only to be hunted down by HMS *Kent* and *Glasgow* and sunk on 14 March 1915 off Juan Fernandez Island.

6 The most famous raider of
them all: SMS *Emden*. The
sister ship of the *Dresden*,
the *Emden* displaced 4340
tonnes (fully loaded), had a
maximum speed of 26 knots,
mounted ten 4.1in guns in
single mounts plus two
torpedo tubes, and had a
crew of 350 men.

7 The *Emden's* area of
operation was the Indian
Ocean, notably the Bay of
Bengal. On 22 September
1914 the oil storage facilities
at Madras were shelled at a
range of 3000m (3300yd) in
a highly successful night
action that was a stinging
blow to British prestige.

8 The *Emden's* career came
to an end on 9 November,
when she was trapped by
HMAS *Sydney* off the Cocos
Islands. The *Sydney's* 6in
guns (depicted here) were
too much for the *Emden*.

9 The wreck of the *Emden*,
run ashore by her captain
after a fierce fight in which
over half her crew became
casualties. In just over three
months the *Emden* had sunk
16 British ships.

10 The crew of the *Emden*.
Her commander, Captain
von Müller, earned his
enemies' respect for his skill
and chivalry.

Battle of the Falklands

1 HMS *Inflexible* at sea. Along with the other two 'Invincible'-class units – *Invincible* and *Indomitable* – the *Inflexible* was one of the new and controversial battlecruisers. The battlecruiser mounted a similar armament to the dreadnought battleship (eight 12in guns on the 'Invincible'-class), had a faster turn of speed but was forced to accept the penalty of limited armour protection. Following the British defeat at Coronel HMS *Invincible* and HMS *Inflexible* were dispatched south under Admiral Sturdee to deal with the German East Asia Squadron.

2 The 'County'-class armoured cruiser HMS *Kent* was one of the smaller ships in Sturdee's squadron. While the battlecruisers fought it out with the *Scharnhorst* and the *Gneisenau,* HMS *Kent* sank the light cruiser SMS *Nürnberg.*

3 SMS *Scharnhorst*, the 11,685-tonne 'name' ship of her class, which included the *Gneisenau*. Armed with eight 8in guns the *Scharnhorst* was the crack gunnery ship of the German Navy.

4 SMS *Gneisenau* leaving port for an ocean-going voyage. The 'Scharnhorst'-class represented a good mix of armour protection, speed and firepower.

5 SMS *Nürnberg*, a light cruiser of the 'Dresden'-class, capable of 26 knots and armed with ten 4.1in guns. The *Dresden* outdistanced the British cruisers, but the *Nürnberg* was caught and sunk.

6 A photograph taken from the *Invincible* at the end of the battle, 8 December 1914, shows HMS *Inflexible* picking up survivors from the *Gneisenau*. The *Scharnhorst* went down with flags flying and her entire crew of 770 men, including Admiral von Spee.

7 Smoke belches from her funnels as HMS *Invincible* charges after the German East Asia Squadron upon making contact off the Falkland Islands. The British battlecruisers had a 5-knot advantage over the German cruisers.

8 Royal Marines and crew members of the *Kent* survey the damage to the upper deck from the 4.1in shells of the *Nürnberg*. The Battle of the Falklands was notable for the accuracy of German gunnery and the resolute spirit in which the Germans fought a hopeless contest.

War in the North Sea

1 A remarkable photograph of the last moments of the 15,750-tonne SMS *Blücher:* her 8.2in guns point defiantly skyward as survivors scramble down the hull and into the water. On 24 January 1915 Admiral Hipper had been authorised to make a sortie across the Dogger Bank in the North Sea but his force was caught by Admiral Beatty's battlecruisers. As Hipper's squadron fled for safety the *Blücher* became the sacrificial rearguard, taking the full force of the British battlecruiser's guns.

2 Beatty's battlecruisers come under fire as they close the range on Hipper's ships at Dogger Bank. Although a victory for the Royal Navy in numerical terms, British signalling errors and poor gunnery allowed the German squadron (with the exception of the *Blücher*) to escape to the safety of their North Sea havens.

3 A Zeppelin of the German Navy flies over a 'Kaiser'-class battleship. The Zeppelin was seen as a solution to the problem of long-range naval reconnaissance. In practice, however, despite unprecedented radio warning of enemy movements, the fog of war persisted.

4 Hit by a mine, the 23,370-tonne HMS *Audacious* sinks off the north coast of Ireland, 27 October 1914. One of the Royal Navy's latest battleships, her loss encouraged respect for the naval mine.

5 Deep in the bowels of the ship, coal is brought from the bunkers to the stokers, whose job was to feed the vast steam boilers.

6 Caught on the surface, a British C-class submarine comes under fire from German seaplanes off Harwich. The *C-25*'s hull was damaged early in the engagement, and, unable to dive, crew members fought back against the German planes with the submarine's Lewis machine gun. The commander, Lieutenant Bell, was killed, along with five of his crew. *C-25* survived the attack, however, and was towed back to Harwich by a mine-laying submarine.

Battle of Jutland
Clash of the dreadnoughts

1 British warships commanded by Admiral Sir David Beatty come under attack at the beginning of the Battle of Jutland, 31 May 1916.

2 A German salvo straddles a 'Birmingham'-class cruiser. At a purely tactical level the battle was noteworthy for the quality of German gunnery and the superior penetrative power of their armour-piercing shells over those of the British.

3 The British Grand Fleet races to catch the German High Seas Fleet at Jutland. Jellicoe's force comprised 24 battleships with a full escort of destroyers and cruisers.

4 *Derfflinger*, the crack gunnery ship of Hipper's battlecruiser squadron, had the measure of Beatty's battlecruisers: at 1626 hours a combined salvo from *Derfflinger* and *Seydlitz* blew up HMS *Queen Mary*, and at 1834 one of her 12in shells dealt a mortal blow to *Invincible*.

5 The British battleship *Royal Oak* at full speed, elevating her eight 15in guns. A 'Royal Sovereign'-class battleship, she displaced 31,750 tonnes and was one of the most powerful warships in service at Jutland, being fast, well-armed and well-protected.

6 HMS *Invincible* was engaged in close action with *Derfflinger* when she was struck amidships by a 12in shell; this entered the starboard turret and ignited the midship turrets' magazine, holding 50 tonne of cordite. The explosion broke the ship in half and killed all but six of the 1031-man crew.

7 The bows and stern of *Invincible* lie clear of the surface while HMS *Badger* picks up the six survivors on the target raft.

8 The German battlecruiser *Seydlitz* burning low in the water after Jutland.

War on the southern flank
The Mediterranean theatre

1 The Austro-Hungarian battleship *Saenkt Stefan* begins to go under after hitting an Italian mine, 10 June 1918.

2 The Austrian torpedo-boat *Wildfang* steaming 'full speed ahead' in the Adriatic. The enclosed nature of the Adriatic Sea gave increased prominence to smaller vessels such as torpedo-boats while increasing the vulnerability of larger warships.

3 The 15in guns of 'A' and 'B' turrets on the HMS *Queen Elizabeth*. Commissioned in 1915, the *Queen Elizabeth* was the 'name' ship of her class, which were considered to be the finest battleships afloat. After taking part in the bombardment of Turkish batteries at Gallipoli. *Queen Elizabeth* was withdrawn to home waters.

4 An aerial view of the aftermath of a sea-battle in the Adriatic. Austrian coastal vessels come to the support of the *Novara*, limping back to port after an engagement with Anglo-Italian forces. The Austrian fleet was firmly blockaded at Pola, but U-boats operating out from Cattaro hunted freely in the Mediterranean.

5 The white puff of smoke below her tall foremast indicates a hit on the cruiser *Novara*.

6 Lieutenant-Commander Arnauld de la Perière and crew members perch on the conning tower of *U-35*, the most successful U-boat in the history of submarine warfare. *U-35* sank 224 ships during her career, mostly in the Mediterranean.

7 British drifters and trawlers at anchor in Taranto. They formed part of the Otranto Barrage, a semi-continuous line of small craft stretching across the southern Adriatic, intended to prevent the passage of enemy submarines.

Menace in the sea-lanes
Germany's U-boat campaign

1 Crew members of *U-49* watch an Italian sailing vessel go up in flames while on a Mediterranean patrol, 19 March 1918. As each submarine could only carry a limited number of torpedoes, they were saved for armed targets, where the U-boat needed to be submerged to make an attack. Unarmed merchant ships were sunk by gunfire from the surfaced submarine.

2 U-boats await inspection at their base in Kiel, October 1918. In 1914 the German Navy had shown little interest in the submarine, but during the course of the war its potential as a 'war-winner' was realised. The U-boats were able to undermine the Royal Navy's surface supremacy, and they almost severed Britain's vital yet vulnerable lifeline of mercantile trade. As in World War II Germany's U-boat arm was considered an elite within the navy.

3 The power of a torpedo is demonstrated as it scores a direct hit on a merchant vessel. The U-boats sank over 14 million tonnes of Allied shipping during World War I, compared with over 17 million tonnes in World War II.

4 Uniformed in the grey leather jackets and trousers of the U-boat service, German submariners check the engines. The German pioneering of the diesel engine gave their submarines great range, allowing them to operate all over the Atlantic for weeks on end.

5 As the war progressed so U-boat guns increased in size. Here a crew prepares a 15cm gun for firing – this was capable of sinking any type of merchant ship. But by 1917 most sinkings were effected by torpedoes.

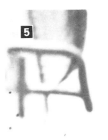

The hunter hunted
Defeat of the U-boats

1 One of the more ingenious methods of combating the U-boat threat was the Q-ship, a 'merchant' vessel fitted with concealed weaponry to turn the tables on an unsuspecting and surfaced U-boat. On the *Hyderabad* a 12-pounder gun (without its concealing shutters) and a Sutton-Armstrong bomb-thrower (revealed inside a cargo hatch) make up part of the ship's forward armament. The Q-ships sank 11 U-boats in all.

2 A routine job in the war against the U-boats, the laying of submarine nets from a British drifter in coastal waters.

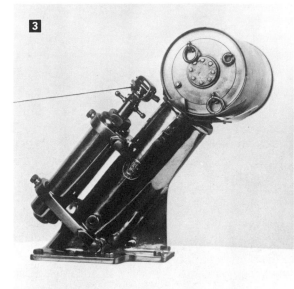

3/4 Cause and effect: a loaded Thornycroft depth-charge-thrower and a depth charge exploding at sea. The depth charge was developed during the war as a means of sinking submerged U-boats whose approximate position could be detected by the use of hydrophones. It was a relatively simple device, a cylindrical canister filled with 136kg (300lb) of TNT, set to explode at a predetermined depth. Although the depth charge had a lethal range of only a few yards, the shock waves it sent through the water could damage a U-boat at a considerable distance. Some 27 U-boats were sunk by depth charges during the course of the war.

5 The U-boats were an extra hazard for the merchantmen in the North Atlantic, who already had to endure dreadful weather conditions. Here a ship's bridge is completely frozen over.

6 A British convoy crossing the Atlantic. In the face of rising losses during early 1917, the convoy system was reluctantly adopted by the Royal Navy. A convoy consisted of a core of slow-moving merchant ships, covered by an escort screen of anti-submarine destroyers and trawlers. The convoy system was a great success, and from May 1917 shipping losses declined, but the U-boats were only finally defeated in 1918.

7 British torpedo-boats and destroyers lay a smoke screen to conceal the movements of a convoy.

Assault from the sea
The Zeebrugge raid

1 A machine-gun post on the Belgian coast, part of a German naval artillery regiment. The Maxim machine guns point seaward in anticipation of a British attack – duly launched against Zeebrugge on 23 April 1918.

2 One of the Hay portable flamethrowers which were used by the 'pyrotechnic brigade' attached to HMS *Vindictive*.

3 One of the raid's objectives was to sever the viaduct connecting the mole at Zeebrugge to the mainland. For this purpose, the British submarine *C-3* was packed with explosives and sent to ram it. This photograph, taken the day after the raid, shows the gap made by *C-3*.

4 HMS *Vindictive* on her return to Dover. During the raid she successfully laid herself alongside the mole, landing a party of men to deal with the German guns which commanded the entrances to the estuary. The *Vindictive* was a light cruiser of 5790 tonnes armed with ten 6in guns and specially prepared to withstand close-quarters gunfire.

5 An aerial photograph of the entrance to the Bruges Canal at Zeebrugge at low tide, showing the sunken *Thetis*, *Intrepid* and *Iphigenia*. These three obsolete vessels were detailed to sink themselves in the canal entrance, blocking it against the U-boats that came down the canal from the base of the Flanders U-boat flotillas at Bruges, before slipping out into the North Sea shipping lanes. That all three ships managed to scuttle themselves in the right positions was a major achievement, although it was subsequently discovered that U-boats were able to slip past the wrecks at high tide.

6 The commander and officers of the German detachment on the mole parade with their decorations at an awards ceremony. Both sides fought with determination.

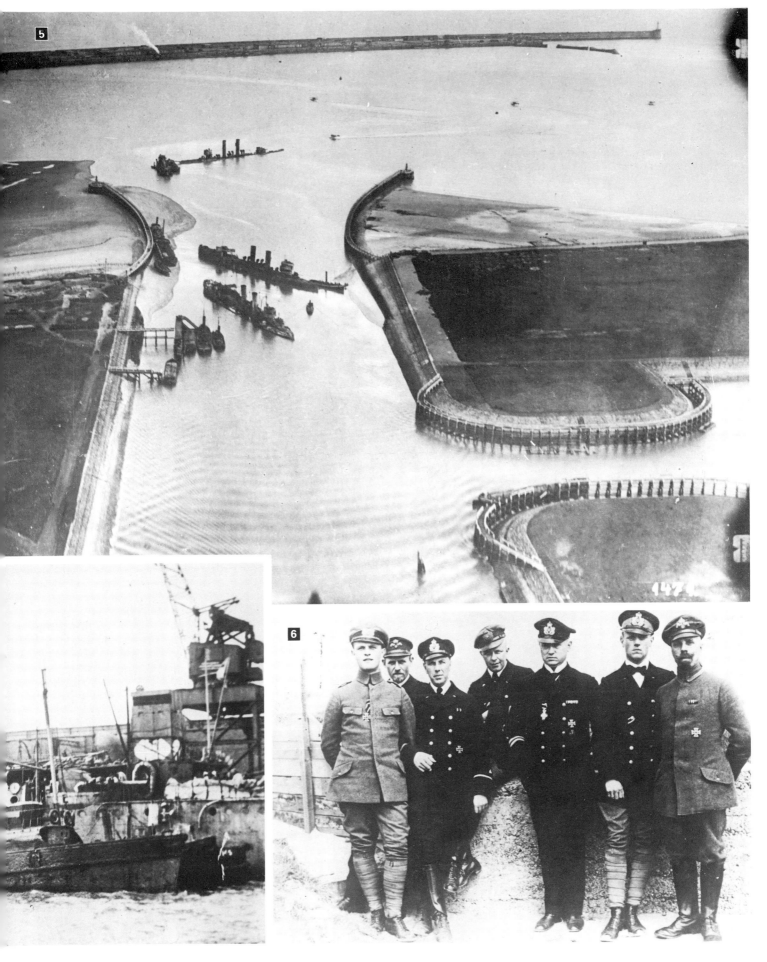

Chapter 7 Allied failure in the West

Above: General Otto von Below commanded the Austro-German Fourteenth Army which spearheaded the assault at Caporetto, October 1917. His forces broke through the Italian line, capturing vast numbers of confused Italian troops.

The cost of the great battles of Verdun and the Somme profoundly shocked the governments of France and Britain: the scale of military effort and loss of so many men were without historical precedent, and yet, as 1916 drew to an end, the net result was apparently deadlock once again. Demands for change were in the air. In France, Joffre was replaced as Commander-in-Chief by General Robert Nivelle, an artillery general who had established a reputation for efficient and successful operations in the French counter-attacks at Verdun. In Britain, the Prime Minister, H.H. Asquith, was replaced by David Lloyd George on 7 December. Always mistrustful of the military, Lloyd George sought to reverse the 'Western' strategy of the Chief of the Imperial General Staff, Sir William Robertson, and of Sir Douglas Haig, by advocating an all-out attempt to crush Austria in 1917.

General Nivelle thought otherwise: he planned a major French offensive in Champagne supported by a British attack around Arras. Nivelle proclaimed that the battle would be won in 48 hours, by an attack of some 1,200,000 men against the German line along the *Chemin des Dames*, which overlooked the River Aisne. With over 5000 guns at his disposal Nivelle guaranteed that the German defences would be pulverised into submission. However, the Germans

became aware of his plan and decided to withdraw to the 'Hindenburg Line', a highly fortified defensive system designed to spare their army another Somme. The withdrawal seriously dislocated Nivelle's plans, but he firmly refused to make any changes in them, and the British had to conform despite their misgivings.

The British diversionary attack around Arras opened the Allied offensive. Supported by 3000 guns, the British and Dominion troops went over the top on 9 April. On the first day the strongly defended Vimy Ridge was captured by the Canadian Corps in a brilliant assault. But from then on progress slowed in the face of stiffening German resistance, and the battle came to an end in May, at a cost of over 150,000 casualties to each side.

The Nivelle offensive began on 16 April. The German defence-in-depth had defeated Nivelle's artillery – and the French infantry paid the price. By the afternoon of the first day the offensive had lost its momentum, but the French pressed on for a further ten days, securing limited objectives and capturing over 28,000 Germans in the process. The net result of the offensive was 187,000 French casualties to an estimated German minimum of 163,000. A further casualty was Nivelle himself, replaced by General Henri Pétain, the 'Saviour of Verdun' in 1916.

By the standards of 1915 and 1916 the French casualties were not high; yet the French Army had received a near-fatal blow. Nivelle's promises had raised the army's expectations to a dangerously high level; now these were brutally dashed when it was realised that his attack had failed to penetrate the German line by more than 7km (4 miles). There was widespread demoralisation, and mutiny was in the air. On 3 May, men of an infantry division refused to go back into the trenches. By the end of June units in over 50 divisions had refused to obey orders.

The situation looked desperate indeed, but with Pétain as Commander-in-Chief order was slowly restored. Ringleaders were shot (55 official executions; there is no record of unofficial cases) but Pétain chiefly relied on remedying the legitimate grievances of the rank-and-file by providing proper leave, food, rest etc. By late August the French Army was once again in a state of discipline, and was able to mount an effective attack at Verdun, followed by another in Champagne in October. However, the mutinies made it necessary for the British Army to assume the main burden of the war in the west.

British GHQ had long ago concluded that the most rewarding area for a British offensive was Flanders – they would have preferred it to the Somme in 1916. The very severe shipping losses of April and May now drew the eyes of the Admiralty and the government towards the U-boat bases at Ostend and Zeebrugge; their elimination seemed, indeed, vital for Britain's survival. The chief action of the BEF in 1917 was thus shaped by the double objective of clearing the Flanders coast, and forcing the Germans out of western Flanders altogether by cutting their railway communications in the neighbourhood of Roulers, northeast of Ypres. Such a success would

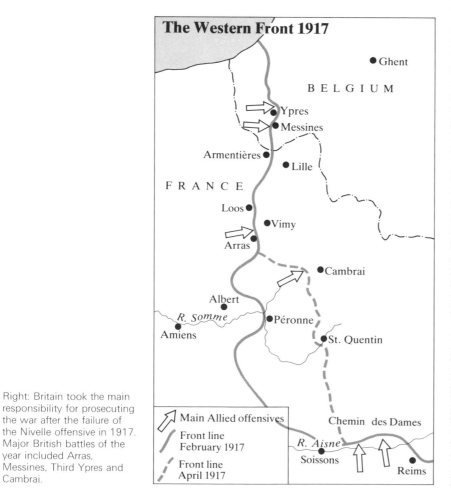

The Western Front 1917

● Ghent

BELGIUM

Ypres
Messines

Armentières ● Lille

FRANCE

Loos ●
● Vimy
Arras

● Cambrai

Albert
R. Somme
Amiens
● Péronne
● St. Quentin

Chemin des Dames

R. Aisne
Soissons
Reims

⇗ Main Allied offensives
〜 Front line February 1917
- - - Front line April 1917

Right: Britain took the main responsibility for prosecuting the war after the failure of the Nivelle offensive in 1917. Major British battles of the year included Arras, Messines, Third Ypres and Cambrai.

Above: The arrogant Italian Commander-in-Chief, General Cadorna. His complacency was a factor in the disastrous Italian defeat at Caporetto, and he was replaced by General Diaz.

Below: General Robert Nivelle gained a reputation as a 'successful' soldier during the final Verdun counter-attacks. Replacing Joffre as Commander-in-Chief, he assured the exhausted French that they would have an easy victory in 1917. His rash promises led to the French Army mutinies of 1917, but his replacement, General Pétain, slowly restored the shattered army to combat effectiveness.

have the further advantage of putting an end to the notorious and costly Ypres Salient.

The first stage of a Flanders offensive had to be the securing of Ypres itself by the capture of the Messines Ridge south of the town. Preparations for this had begun a year earlier, with the digging of mines under the Ridge. The tunnelling companies of General Sir Herbert Plumer's Second Army had now completed 19 of these, containing around 450,000kg (1,000,000lb) of high explosive. Plumer's attack at Messines on 7 June opened with the explosion of the mines, causing a virtual earthquake, followed immediately by a hurricane bombardment of over 2000 guns. The infantry advance was a complete success; the Ridge was taken according to plan, and counter-attacks easily repelled. It was a triumph for the Second Army.

Unfortunately, Haig now transferred the main attack northward to General Gough's Fifth Army, while also preparing an amphibious operation under Rawlinson to take Ostend. Preparations for these operations took a long time; in the end the amphibious attack was abandoned, and Gough's first step was not made until 31 July – just in time to founder in an unusually wet August. Against the mud and the concrete pill-box defences, Gough's men, in scenes of intense misery, could achieve little. Belatedly, Haig turned again to Plumer, but this brought yet more delay.

Plumer's methodical preparations were completed by 20 September, when the first of three step-by-step limited advances took place. Each was a triumphant success in good weather, spearheaded by Australians and New Zealanders. The third, at Broodseinde on 4 October, was especially punishing for the Germans. A British breakthrough seemed imminent, reserves were few and the morale of the German defenders at a low ebb. Plumer planned further efforts on similar lines, but on 7 October cold, drenching rain set in again, and slowly the battle foundered in a porridge of mud in which guns, mules and sometimes wounded men sank without trace. The last advance, on 6 November, was the capture by the Canadians of a brick-coloured stain in the mud which had been the village of Passchendaele, and which gave the battle its name. The offensive ended on 12 November, by which time British casualties amounted to some 245,000 (plus 8500 French); German losses are not known – they called Passchendaele 'the greatest martyrdom of the war'.

While the Flanders battle raged, the Germans stripped the remainder of their front in the west to the minimum. Taking advantage of this, the French attack in Champagne on 23 October captured over 11,000 prisoners. Elsewhere, October ended badly for the Allies; Italy had fought two hard battles of attrition, the Tenth Battle of the Isonzo in May, costing 157,000 men in just over three weeks, and the Eleventh Battle from 18 August to 12 September, costing 165,000. This left the Italian Army in a badly weakened condition. The Austrians, with some German aid, promptly launched an offensive of their own, later named after its focal point, the village of Caporetto.

A short whirlwind bombardment announced the opening of the attack, on 24 October. Crack Austrian and German mountain units, pressing forward through snowstorms and low cloud, tore the Italian defences apart. Communications broke down, and the Italian Army collapsed; hundreds of thousands of men deserted, and 275,000 surrendered. Battle casualties numbered only 40,000, but 2500 guns were captured. The Italian retreat continued to the Piave River, some 100km (60 miles) from Caporetto; here they were able to stand on prepared positions against the now exhausted Austrians, while six French and five British divisions came to their support from the Western Front. By 12 November the fighting was over; it had been a severe and shocking blow to Allied hopes.

Since September 1917, British GHQ had been planning a further attack on the Western Front, to clinch the success that was still hoped for in Flanders. It was to take the form of a surprise attack by General Sir Julian Byng's Third Army, at Cambrai. Uncratered ground offered an opportunity for the mass use of tanks (impossible in Flanders) and surprise was to be ensured by 'predicted shooting' – starting the bombardment without previous registration of the artillery – an innovation on the British front, though already pioneered with success by the Germans in the east.

At 0620 hours on 20 November, 1000 guns opened fire with a single crash on the unsuspecting Germans, and 378 fighting tanks rolled forward through the autumn mist. By midday the British had penetrated some 6km (4 miles) through the forward defences of the Hindenburg Line. But the cavalry which had been intended to exploit the success completely failed to do so, and the Germans continued to hold strong positions on the flanks of the British advance. Furthermore, half the tanks were out of action at the end of the day, chiefly due to mechanical failure. Once more a battle degenerated into trench-to-trench fighting, for which the British had no reserves (five divisions having gone to Italy).

On 30 November it was the turn of the Germans to spring a surprise: a counter-attack spearheaded by 'Storm Troops', specially trained attack groups, using the tactic of 'infiltration' to find and exploit the weak points of the British line and dislocate it by deep penetrations and encirclement. This was the debut of that tactic, and, like the British combination of predicted shooting and tanks, it worked well. By 5 December, when the battle ended, the British had lost half their gains of ground, and both sides had suffered about 45,000 casualties.

The failure to win a decision in Flanders, the U-boat campaign, Russia's collapse, the heavy defeat of Italy and now the Cambrai setback made a gloomy end to a year of persistent disappointment for the Western Allies.

Arras and Vimy Ridge

1 A file of British infantry crosses an old communication trench – now converted into shelters with corrugated iron and waterproof sheets – near the Feuchy crossroads. Alongside the infantry are some of the other elements of the British Army in 1917: a battery of 18-pounders (deployed in their standard battlefield echelon), tanks and, in the distance, cavalry.

2 A 12in howitzer and shells under camouflage netting, Arras, April 1917. The battle was preceded by a week-long bombardment. The quality of the shells was far better than it had been on the Somme, and the new '106' fuze made its debut, designed to cut wire more effectively. During 1916 and 1917 the British gunners were learning and developing their craft, so that by 1918 the Royal Artillery was to dictate the course of the fighting.

3 Shells explode in the distance as British wounded are treated at a dressing station. Intended as a short, limited battle, the Arras offensive was prolonged until 23 May to provide aid for the French, who had suffered badly in their own (Nivelle) offensive. Total British casualties were 158,660 men for the period from 8 April to 23 May.

4 A barbed-wire entanglement in front of the Hindenburg Line, to which the Germans retired in the spring of 1917.

5 Canadian infantrymen gain the crest of Vimy Ridge on the first day of their offensive, 9 April 1917. The Ridge was the dominant tactical feature to the north of Arras and its capture was an essential first step in the overall plan. The four divisions of the Canadian Corps numbered around 100,000 men; in securing Vimy Ridge they suffered 9937 casualties but captured over 4000 Germans and 54 guns. Gaining the Ridge was a considerable tactical achievement, and was a source of pride for the Canadians.

6 British troops in Arras celebrate their capture of Monchy-le-Preux on 11 April. They are being withdrawn from the battlefield in commandeered omnibuses – a possible reason for their enthusiasm. The major gains of the Arras offensive were made in the first week's fighting.

Trench warfare
Defending the line

3 A crack German sniper team operating on the Western Front, 1917. While the sniper would fire the deadly shot, his observer would select the target and check where the bullet landed, verifying hits and correcting misses. The Germans had a most professional approach to sniping, adopting a system in which the snipers worked in the same sector over a period of months, gaining familiarity with the enemy trench system. This contrasted with the British, whose snipers were rotated at intervals along with their battalions. Again, unlike the British sniper, the German had ready access to telescopic sights and bullet-proof steel loopholes, although the latter were eventually dispensed with, since they revealed the presence of a sniper to the enemy.

4 Armed with 0.3in Springfield rifles, these US Army snipers are kitted out in full camouflage suits, considered useful for operating in vegetation.

5 Trench raids and night patrols were regular events in the struggle to establish ascendancy over no man's land. This patrol near Cambrai in January 1917 is notable for the use of winter camouflage suits.

6 An early-morning scene on the Somme, as the attack on Thiepval begins, 15 September 1916. The German front-line troops are sending up SOS flares to prompt their artillery to reply to the British assault.

7 Under shellfire, soldiers of the Cameronians (Scottish Rifles) leap out of their forward sap at the start of a daylight raid near Arras, 24 March 1917. During the war there was considerable controversy as to the value of trench raids; their ostensible aim was to gain intelligence of the enemy units and precise details of enemy fortifications. The raiders' prime objective was to take prisoners, since their uniforms, equipment and possessions could provide valuable intelligence. On the debit side, raiding parties often suffered heavy casualties and invited retaliation.

Defeat and demoralisation
The Nivelle offensive

1 The first wave of the attack: French troops of a colonial corps advance towards the German trenches on the *Chemin des Dames* in April 1917. French artillery fire is visible on the horizon. German positions on the *Chemin des Dames* had been greatly improved in anticipation of the French offensive, and comprised a series of lightly held outposts behind which were three systems stretching back to a depth of around 7000m (7700yd). Extensive use was made of tunnels to protect the troops from artillery fire and to allow the speedy reinforcement of threatened sectors. German defensive preparations were altogether better than was asserted by General Nivelle.

2 An explosive barrage smashes into a German front-line trench. Impressive though this looked. French intelligence of the German positions was poor, and they escaped the full force of the preliminary bombardments.

3 A long line of French infantry marches up to the front. Nivelle had promised outright victory to his men and expectations were high. The first day of the offensive (16 April) saw some limited gains. The French troops pressed home their attacks with the greatest vigour but the German defence was able to absorb the French thrusts, which foundered on the German second line.

4 Wearing gas masks, a French gun-crew fires some of the 11,000,000 shells which preceded the Nivelle offensive. Although an impressive figure, it was not to translate into results on the battlefield; the barrage was spread out over too wide a front, around 40km (25 miles).

5 French infantrymen march down a muddy track in northern France. Although the spring offensive of 1917 compared favourably with those of 1915 – in the period 16–30 April 1917 the French lost 118,000 men, but captured over 20,000 and 150 guns – Nivelle's promises had raised French hopes to unrealistic levels. With the dawning of reality came disillusionment and then mutiny.

Underground attack
Messines Ridge

1 The Battle of Messines Ridge was a limited engagement, designed to secure the high ground to the south of Ypres. The assault was preceded by a 12-day artillery bombardment; here 8in Mk V howitzers bombard German trenches, 25 May 1917.

2 Deep underground, a tunnelling party makes repairs. The most noteworthy feature of the battle preparations were the 24 mines laid under the German positions. The mines contained 500 tonnes of high explosive and were simultaneously detonated at dawn on 7 June.

3 General Plumer's Second Army was entrusted with the attack and his preparations were typically thorough. Here men of the 13th Brigade study a large contour model of their battlefield objectives.

4 The view across the Douve Valley, with the town of Messines – on the high ground in the distance – undergoing heavy shelling.

5 A mine going up. Although five of the mines at Messines were not detonated, the other 19 destroyed the German front-line positions in a giant thunderclap, leaving the survivors too dazed to offer serious resistance.

6 The remains of Oosttaverne Wood and the wrecked German trenches captured by the British on the first day of the offensive. Besides the mines, the German defenders had to contend with a barrage of gas shells into their trenches. There was a fight for the German second line, and a counter-attack was mounted, but British artillery dispersed this danger.

7 German prisoners taken during the battle. The British, Australian and New Zealand divisions of the Second Army captured 7500 men and 67 guns, and inflicted a further 17,500 casualties for a loss of 17,000 of their own men. Messines was a triumphant vindication of the strategy of precise application of devastating firepower.

Passchendaele
Graveyard in the mud

1 British gunners prepare a 6in howitzer in support of the struggle for Pilckem, August 1917. Featuring a highly efficient recoil mechanism, this howitzer was capable of firing a 45kg (100lb) shell to a maximum of 8700m (9500yd).

2 Infantrymen make a dash towards a German strongpoint during the Fifth Army's attack on Pilckem. German defences around Ypres had been improved before the main battle began on 31 July, and here the British infantry encountered the small concrete outposts nicknamed 'pillboxes'. Cunningly sited and able to resist anything but direct hits from heavy artillery, the pillboxes helped to check the British advance.

3 Identification papers are collected from a dead British soldier, Château Wood, October 1917. The administration of millions of men in a foreign country was a formidable task which was carried out with remarkable efficiency. This included the identification and burial of the dead.

4 The Third Battle of Ypres – or Passchendaele, as it became known to the troops – became synonymous with mud. A stretcher party of seven men struggles back with a wounded comrade, August 1917. The summer of 1917 received exceptionally heavy rainfall; the August figures were more than double the average.

5 Dead German troops, victims of the pre-attack bombardment of 31 July 1917. By 1917 the British Army was at last able to support its offensives with adequate numbers of guns. German accounts invariably speak with horror of the effect of major British artillery barrages.

6 The negative consequence of the ten-day-long bombardment, which saw 65,000 tonnes of metal thrown at the Germans, was the destruction of the surface drainage system. The combination of heavy rainfall, low-lying marshy ground and heavy bombardment transformed much of the Ypres battlefield into an impassable quagmire. Third Ypres came to a close on 10 November, a few days after the capture of the village of Passchendaele, some 8km (5 miles) from the start-line.

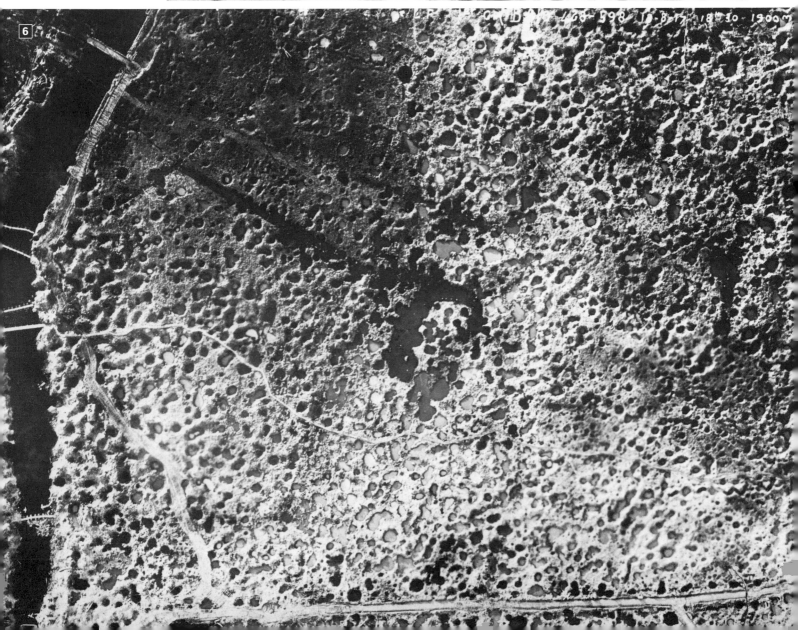

The tanks

1 The French Renault FT17 light tank demonstrates its climbing abilities on French Army manoeuvres. The most successful French tank of the war, the FT17 was a blueprint for subsequent tank design, with its revolving turret-mounted 37mm gun.

2 The *Char d'Assaut* Schneider was a less than successful armoured fighting vehicle (poor cross-country mobility combined with vulnerability to smallarms fire), but it at least gave the French experience of operating tanks in battlefield conditions.

3 A *Char d'Assaut* St Chamond passes through a wood during fighting by the River Oise. Its main armament was a forward-mounted 75mm gun.
-Spread 7, Page 120(B)

4 A British Whippet or Medium Tank Mk A moves up towards the front line in the Somme region, summer 1918. Capable of a maximum speed of 13km/h (8mph) the Whippet was specifically designed to act in a cavalry role, exploiting any breakthroughs. This it did with some success in the great battles of 1918.

5 German troops dash out from the shelter of Germany's only wartime tank design, the A7V *Stürmpanzerwagen*. Weighing 33 tonnes, the ungainly A7V had a crew of up to 18 men and was armed with a 57mm main gun and six machine guns. Slow, unstable, and unable to cross rough terrain, the A7V was not a success.

6 'Mother' negotiates a steep incline during proving trials, January 1916. The trench stalemate was a great stimulus to the development of armoured 'landships'. During 1915 experiments were carried out with a variety of designs, the most successful evolving through the caterpillar-tracked 'Little Willie' into 'Mother'. 'Mother' became the prototype Tank MkI (the name derived from the codename 'water tank'), recognisable by its distinctive lozenge-shaped tracks and the sponsons on each side of the tank, each mounting a 6-pounder gun. Reliability and mobility were major problems with this design.

7 British MkV tanks of the US Army under shellfire, October 1918. Although this appears to be an exceptional 'action' photograph, its authenticity remains in doubt.

Battle of Cambrai
Attack and counter-attack

1 Preparations for Cambrai; a tank train awaits dispatch to forward de-training railheads. The bundles of fascines carried on top of the tanks were for dropping into deep obstacles such as enemy trenches. The importance of Cambrai as a tank battle was that for the first time tanks were used in substantial numbers.

2 Tanks pass captured 7.7cm field guns, 23 November 1917. The 378 front-line tanks had performed impressively on the first day, but casualties and breakdowns reduced their numbers to only 199 by the following morning.

3 The element of surprise had played an important part in the tactical considerations governing the British plan of attack. The tanks had been assembled in conditions of utmost secrecy, the guns fired no preliminary registration shots and the whole artillery barrage was confined to the morning of the attack. The Germans were caught completely unawares and the British captured 7000 men and 170 guns in a matter of hours. Here, British troops salvage German smallarms, 22 November.

4 Men of the Inniskilling Fusiliers guard a newly captured German trench on the first day of the battle, which saw a then unequalled penetration of 6300m (7000yd) in some places.

5 German troops set up a Maxim machine gun in the firing bay of a forward trench. The German counter-attack was launched on 30 November and threw the weakened British units back almost to their original line of 20 November. German success was largely due to the introduction of specially formulated infiltration tactics.

6 Men of a German grenadier patrol demonstrate their skills for the camera, while a messenger dog brings up supplies of disc grenades.

Battle of Caporetto
An Italian disaster

1 Austrian mountain troops cut through a simple barbed-wire entanglement barring an Alpine mountain path. By the autumn of 1917 the attritional war in the Alps and along the River Isonzo was taking its toll of both sides. For the Italians, the 11 battles of the Isonzo had caused them 600,000 casualties for almost no territorial gain. This had engendered a profound war-weariness among both the army and the Italian people. On the other hand, the Austrian commanders on the Italian front were losing confidence in the ability of their troops to withstand further Italian offensives, and appealed to their German ally for help in mounting their own offensive.

2 An Austrian trench mortar in action. Some 2000 guns and mortars were dragged forward for the Battle of Caporetto.

3 Troops of the Austro-German Fourteenth Army cross the Isonzo, ready to assault the Italian positions under fire on the far bank. Von Below's Fourteenth Army comprised 16 divisions (seven of which were German), which had little trouble in breaking through the Italian line.

4 Kitted-out in gas masks, Austrian troops make ready their 8mm Schwarzlose machine gun. The Austrian divisions of the Fourteenth Army were sound formations and like their fellow German divisions were well-equipped with guns, ammunition and essential supplies. Austro-German tactics for the offensive (named Caporetto after the small town opposite the Fourteenth Army's position) centred upon infiltration past enemy strongpoints and the rapid exploitation of any promising breakthrough.

5 German Storm Troops practise small-unit tactics, a few days before the opening of the battle on 24 October. Alongside the Mauser carbines are Danish-manufactured 8mm M1903 Madsen light machine guns. In most respects the German Army was well-served by its arms manufacturers, but the failure to produce a true LMG was a noteworthy exception. The cut-down version of the standard Maxim, the 08/15, remained a heavy, water-cooled gun, and so the Germans tended to use Madsens, or captured British Lewis guns.

6 German transport wagons wind their way through an Alpine pass, following up the rapid advance of the German mountain regiments. The way in which the Italian Second Army disintegrated under German attack came as a great surprise, even to the Germans. Italian casualties told the story: 40,000 killed and wounded and 275,000 taken prisoner.

The Americans arrive

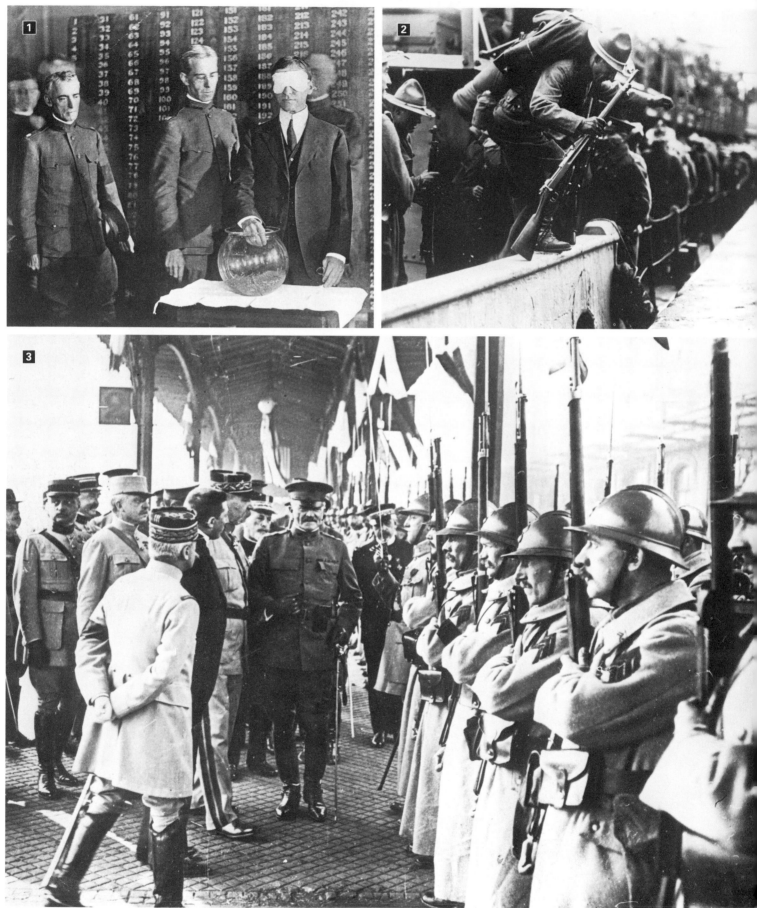

1 The lottery of conscription: a blindfold volunteer pulls out the numbers which will translate into call-up papers for the new recruits to America's armed forces. The draft was far from universally popular and evasion was common, but an army was rapidly assembled and a final total of 2,084,000 men were embarked for service in Europe.

2 American troops disembark in France before dispatch to training camps to familiarise them with the conditions of the Western Front.

3 Commander of the US Army in France, General Pershing inspects a guard of honour on his arrival in Boulogne. Pershing was determined to keep complete control of his troops so that they could operate as an autonomous army, rather than follow the Allied proposal that they be deployed by divisions, wherever most needed, under Allied direction.

4 Foodstuffs and other supplies are unloaded on a French quayside, part of the chain that kept in being the rapidly expanding US Army. Unlike the situation in World War II, the Americans in this war relied heavily on the French and British for their weapons and equipment. The US Army of 1917–18 was essentially an army of riflemen; artillery, aircraft, transport and tanks were supplied by the Allies.

5 American troops make themselves comfortable in a sandbag dug-out. By the end of 1917, the strain of the war had begun to erode the morale of the Allied armies; American enthusiasm was in marked contrast to the more weary and cautious attitude of the French and British.

6 Under the scrutiny of French soldiers, an American recruit shows off his 0.3in Springfield rifle. For the most part US troops fought alongside the French, the bulk of their front-line divisions being deployed on both sides of the Verdun fortress. By September 1918 the American forces were ready for independent action and achieved a notable success in reducing the St Mihiel Salient.

Chapter 8 The war in the air

Above: Commander of the German Air Force, General von Hoeppner, inspects a fighter squadron on the Western Front. To his right is the fighter ace, Manfred von Richthofen, who shot down at least 80 enemy aircraft before his own death in the air in April 1918.

Below: Some of Germany's best aircraft were designed by the Dutchman Anthony Fokker, seen here by a Fokker M16. The Fokker Triplane was one of Richthofen's favourite planes, while the Fokker DVII was considered by many to be the best fighter of the war.

Between 1903 (when the Wright brothers made their first flight) and 1914 the armies and navies of Europe experimented with aircraft as weapons of war; aviation enthusiasts made large claims for the new invention, but doubts remained among the military as to its function and usefulness. As well as aeroplanes, the Germans soon developed the powered airship (*Zeppelin*), and they had five available for service on the Western Front in 1914. It soon became obvious that reconnaissance was the aircraft's role in that conflict. Cavalry was unable to cope with the new battlefield conditions; an aircraft, by contrast, could survey great distances from its vantage point in the sky, and with a speed of around 100km/h (60mph) could report back quickly. It was pilots of the Royal Flying Corps (RFC) and French air service who spotted the German First Army's key change of direction towards Paris which led to the Battle of the Marne in 1914.

As soon as the reconnaissance aircraft became established, counter-measures were applied; the need for information was balanced by the need to deny it to the enemy. At first, the crews of opposing machines waved in mutual acknowledgment, but this innocent chivalry was soon dispensed with. First with revolvers and rifles, then with machine guns, the airmen engaged each other. In these primitive early combats lay the genesis of the 'fighter' and the concept of air superiority.

A necessary prerequisite for a true fighter aircraft was a forward-firing machine gun, but a major obstruction in tractor-screw machines was the arc of the propeller. The problem was solved in two stages: first, the French team of Garros and Saulnier fitted deflector plates on the propeller itself, to prevent it from being shot away. Then, in April 1915, the Dutchman Anthony Fokker presented the Germans with an interrupter gear, a complex mechanical system which stopped the gun firing momentarily as the propeller blade passed in front of it. In the hands of pilots such as Max Immelmann and Oswald Boelcke, the *Eindecker* (monoplane) created the legend of the

'Fokker Scourge' of 1915. The development of the fighter brought with it a new breed of airman, the skilled and ruthless 'aces' who roamed the skies of France and Flanders seeking to increase their tally of enemies shot down.

The advantage in air combat swung from one side to the other as aviation developed. The German supremacy of 1915 and early 1916 was countered by the arrival of better Allied aircraft, notably the French Nieuport XVII and the British DH2. Advantages in numbers, tactics and organisation were important in the battle for aerial superiority, but it was always the quality of the aircraft that ultimately decided the issue over the Western Front. In September the first twin-gunned Albatros fighters were deployed in the German Air Service, and proceeded to overwhelm the Allies that autumn and the following spring. In April 1917 – 'Bloody April', as it became known – the RFC reached its lowest ebb; the life expectancy of young, inexperienced pilots was only a matter of days, and morale began to fail. At this point a new generation of British aircraft – the Sopwith Triplane, the SE5a, and the Sopwith Camel, among others – turned the tables in favour of the Allies. Only in the last months of the war did the Germans look like regaining the initiative, with the introduction of the Fokker DVII, but there were not enough to turn the tide.

The 'dog-fighting' exploits of the fighter aces captured the imagination of the public, but the primary role of aircraft throughout the war was the support of ground forces. In trench warfare, dominated by artillery, the airmen played a vital part, their function being to observe enemy entrenchments, artillery and machine-gun positions, and establishments in the rear. Photographic reconnaissance was soon introduced, enabling the minutest details to be incorporated into the trench maps and artillery maps. Air-to-ground communications developed steadily, especially between artillery batteries and spotting aircraft which both located enemy gun positions and guided the gunners' fall of shot onto target.

The advances in air warfare originated mainly on the Western Front, but aerial activity was by no means confined to that theatre. The Russians experimented (not very successfully) with four-engined bombers; the warplanes of Italy and Austria-Hungary flew and fought over the Alps and Adriatic Sea; in Palestine, in 1918, General Allenby's air force turned Turkish retreat into rout. Meanwhile at sea, air observation had become a regular function: aircraft carriers were introduced, and aeroplanes, airships, seaplanes and flying boats all made a significant contribution to anti-U-boat warfare.

The emergence of the aircraft as a multi-role fighting machine was completed by the development of the bomber. The Royal Naval Air Service was an early pioneer of strategic bombing, launching its first air raid with an attack on Zeppelin sheds at Düsseldorf and Cologne on 22 September 1914. Some enterprising airmen began to carry simple missiles such as ball-bearings or darts to throw down on the enemy below, and these were soon replaced by shells, grenades and bombs. The bomber aircraft pro-

gressed along two separate paths: the first, acting in a tactical role in support of ground troops – strafing enemy formations with machine guns and anti-personnel bombs – and the second, performing a strategic function by attacking the enemy far behind the front line.

The early bomber aircraft lacked not only proper aerial bombs, but also bomb-sights; the latter arrived in 1915, when the RFC raided rail communications behind the German lines during the Battle of Loos. The RFC did not have the numbers of aircraft nor the destructive weight of bombs needed to make this really successful, but it nonetheless marked a first attempt at interdiction bombing.

It was Germany that made the first real attempt at a strategic air offensive against the civilian population.

This was done initially with Zeppelin airships and later with specially designed long-range bombers. The first Zeppelin attack on England was launched on 19 January 1915, and was followed by a further 19 raids during the year. Casualties were relatively light (a total of 556 deaths and 1357 injured), but the public outcry was enormous; England had lost its island security and immediate counter-measures were demanded. These were slow in coming, however, as the Zeppelins proved surprisingly hard to shoot down. It was 1916 before a defensive system of anti-aircraft guns, searchlights, barrage balloons and night-fighters had come into service.

The Germans began to phase out their Zeppelin raids in 1916, not so much in response to the British defences but because of the arrival of the superior Gotha and Giant aeroplanes. On 25 May 1917 Folkestone was bombed by Gothas, the first in a series of raids against southeast England over the next 12 months. Again, casualties were few (a total of 835 killed, 1972 injured) but the outraged British public called not only for improved defensive measures but for direct retaliation. An independent air force was created for the bombing of strategic targets in Germany, and by 1918 a start had been made with the Handley Page series of bombers. The Handley Page 0/1500, with its range of nearly 2000km (1240 miles), was capable of reaching Berlin with 1500kg (3300lb) of bombs; only the armistice on 11 November 1918 prevented this true strategic bomber from demonstrating its capabilities.

The importance of aviation in the war was confirmed in Britain by the formation of a separate Service – the Royal Air Force – on 1 April 1918. The growth of the RNAS/RFC/RAF since 1914 had been dramatic, from a handful of men and machines to a highly professional organisation of 293,532 officers and men and 22,000 aircraft – by the end of the war the largest air force in the world.

Aerial reconnaissance
Balloons and scouts

1 A Caquot kite balloon is brought down to its mooring with the aid of a motor winch. This balloon has just completed a stint of observation over British rearward trench lines, looking towards German positions (in the background) around Fricourt in the Somme region. A relatively stable aerial platform, the balloon was an economical method of observing enemy troop movements and providing the gunners with information about their fall of shot.

2 A German aircraft shoots down a French observation balloon over the Western Front. Despite their apparent vulnerability balloons were not easy to destroy, and were sometimes defended by cunningly sited anti-aircraft guns – a potentially fatal trap for inexperienced pilots.

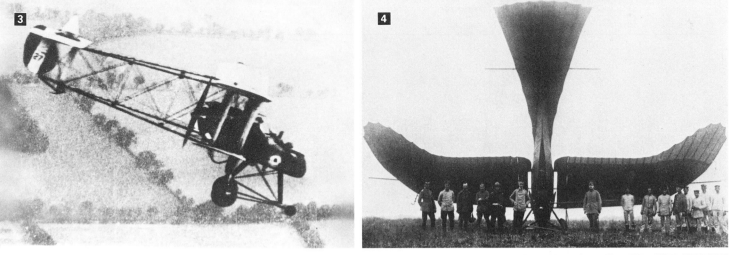

3 Despite its archaic appearance the 'pusher' propelled FE2 represented a serious and largely successful counter to the threat of the Fokker monoplane. The aircraft featured a rear-mounted 120hp engine – giving a maximum speed of 130km/h (82mph) – in front of which was the pilot's seat. The observer/gunner sat in the forward cockpit. One (and later two) Lewis machine guns would be mounted in the forward cockpit, providing the gunner with a completely clear field of fire.

4 A German 'Taube' aircraft reveals its bird-like design, following a landing accident. One example dropped a few bombs on Paris in August 1914, but by then it was obsolete.

5 The delicate lines of the Maurice Farman S7 'Longhorn' can be seen as it comes into land. This early version is fitted with a biplane tail unit.

6 A BE2 prepares for take-off on a simple grass field. In this aircraft the pilot sat in the rear and the observer in the forward cockpit where a Lewis gun was mounted, although its field of fire was severely restricted. Unable to defend itself adequately, the BE2 also suffered from poor performance which gave it top speed of only 115km/h (72mph). Nonetheless its aerial stability and good endurance (over three hours) made it a useful reconnaissance machine.

Zeppelin raids

1 The German military Zeppelin, LZ-77; it carried out raids over Essex in September 1915 but was brought down by Allied gunfire at Revigny in France on 21 February 1916. Throughout 1915 Zeppelins conducted raids over eastern England, causing considerable dismay among the civilian population.

2 Curious French onlookers inspect a Zeppelin after its forced landing at Luneville in France. The 'R'-type had a length of 198m (650ft) and a height of 28m (91ft); it had a maximum speed of 103km/h (64mph) and carried a crew of 19 men.

3 The rear-gunner and observer of a Zeppelin, armed with a 7.92mm 08/15 Maxim machine gun. Cut off from the rest of the crew, he could only communicate with the control car at the forward end of the airship by means of a speaking tube.

4 The pilot's controls in the control car of L-59. In anything other than good weather conditions, piloting a Zeppelin was complex and physically demanding.

5/6/7 A sequence of photographs of a Zeppelin raid over London. By the end of 1915 air-defence measures had steadily improved, and the capital was defended by searchlights, anti-aircraft guns and squadrons of night fighters. Once caught in the beam of a searchlight, the slow-moving and bulky Zeppelin had little chance of escape. Other searchlights would quickly home in on the airship, making it a highly visible target.

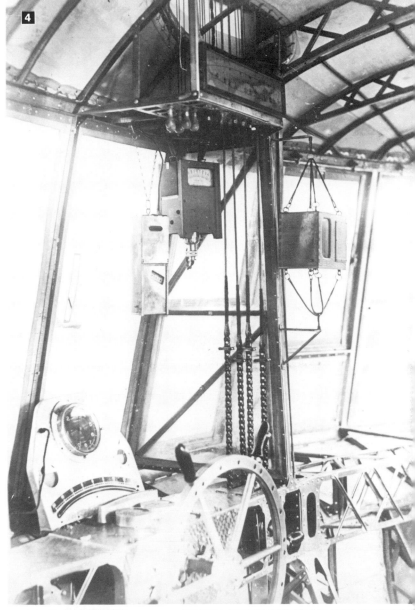

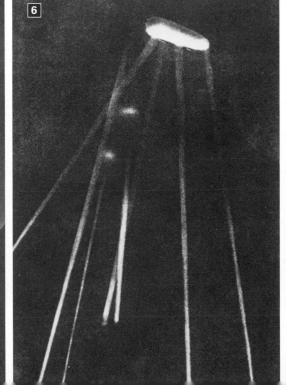

Air combat

1 A mechanic hands over photographic plates to the observer of an RE8 prior to a flight over German lines beyond Arras, February 1918. Armament includes a rear-mounted Lewis gun and a Vickers gun bolted to the port side of the fuselage.

2 On the return of the RE8, a photographic mosaic of enemy positions is made up by the intelligence officer. Photographic reconnaissance did not have the glamour attached to the fighter squadrons, but it was arguably the single most important task undertaken by the RFC/RAF during the war.

3 Wearing gas masks, the crew of a German ground-attack aircraft prepares for a low-level mission against enemy troops and transport.

4 The most manoeuvrable of the Allied fighters, the Sopwith Camel, looping the loop. Although a difficult aeroplane to fly, it was an excellent dogfighter, scoring 2880 confirmed kills during the war – more than any other Allied fighter.

5 As part of the defence of London against the German aerial intruders, balloon aprons were stretched across likely areas of German attack.

6 An unusual view of the pilot (facing camera) and gunner of a French observation aeroplane over Champagne.

7 The cockpit of an SE5a, one of the best of the RFC's fighters on the Western Front. By the standards of later aircraft the instruments of World War I aircraft were very basic, but they provided the pilot with his essential requirements, *i.e.* height, direction and speed. The SE5a was armed with a Vickers gun mounted in the fuselage (to the right of which stands a simple telescopic sight) and a wing-mounted Lewis gun, bolted on to an adjustable mounting.

8 German anti-aircraft defences: a stereoscopic viewfinder plots the range and height of the target for the 3.7cm quick-firing Flak gun, fitted with a side-mounted magazine.

Fighters and aces

1 Hauptmann Oswald Boelcke (40 kills) is acknowledged as the first of the true fighter aces. Rising to eminence with the Fokker EIII monoplane (just visible behind him) he and fellow ace Max Immelmann were prominent in the 'Fokker scourge' of the winter of 1915–16.

2 Lieutenant Charles Nungesser (45 kills) stands beside his Nieuport biplane. Frequently wounded, he flew at every opportunity, sometimes having to be carried to his plane because of unset broken bones.

3 Rittmeister Manfred von Richthofen (right, 80 kills) stands with his brother Lothar in front of a Fokker DR1 Triplane. Von Richthofen, nicknamed the 'Red Baron,' was the war's top-scoring pilot, but was shot down and killed on 21 April 1918.

4 Major Edward 'Mick' Mannock (73 kills) began his career in April 1917 and became the top-scoring British ace. He was also a superb combat leader.

5 Capitaine René Fonck (75 kills) was an outstanding marksman, able to shoot down an opponent with a few well-placed rounds. He flew Spads with the elite French 'Les Cigognes' squadron, and survived the war.

6 Captain Edward Rickenbacker (26 kills) was the top-scoring American ace. He was posted to a fighter squadron in March 1918 and proved to be a natural flyer.

7 Lieutenant-Colonel William 'Billy' Bishop (72 kills) leans on the wing of his Nieuport 17. A Canadian, Bishop began flying as an observer, but after training joined No.60 Squadron in March 1917.

The bombers

1 A British RE8 sets out on a night bombing raid, 23 October 1917. The RE8 was one of the least successful aircraft supplied to the RFC: it was an unforgiving plane to fly, with many dangerous faults.

2 Bombing in its infancy: an observer leans out of his cockpit ready to deliver his 'gift' to the enemy below. Only with the development of proper bomb-sights in 1915 could the bomber be considered a serious weapon of war.

3 The bulk of a Handley Page 0/400 bomber coming into land. The 0/400 was an upgraded 0/100 bomber which had come into operational service towards the end of 1916, although it was only in the last year of the war that they were used to any effect. The 0/400 was powered by two 360hp engines providing a top speed of 156km/h (97mph) and its armament comprised up to five Lewis guns and a maximum bomb load of 907kg (2000lb).

4 Officers of the shortlived Independent Air Force which emerged in 1918 reveal their disparate service origins in the variety of uniforms worn.

5 Italy produced a number of successful bombers including the Caproni Ca 4 which featured this unusual triplane and twin-boom layout. Powered by three 250hp engines, top speed was 150km/h (93mph) and an impressive bombload of up to 900kg (1984lb) could be carried.

6 The Russian four-engined Ilya Muromets bomber was designed by the helicopter pioneer Igor Sikorsky, and when unveiled in January 1914 it was by far the most advanced aircraft of its type.

7 A German Gotha bomber banks away beside the column of smoke rising from its target. The Gotha bombers made a number of daring raids against southeast England in 1917–18.

8 A Gotha GV is loaded with its complement of five 50kg (110lb) bombs alongside the two 100kg (220lb) bombs slung under the fuselage.

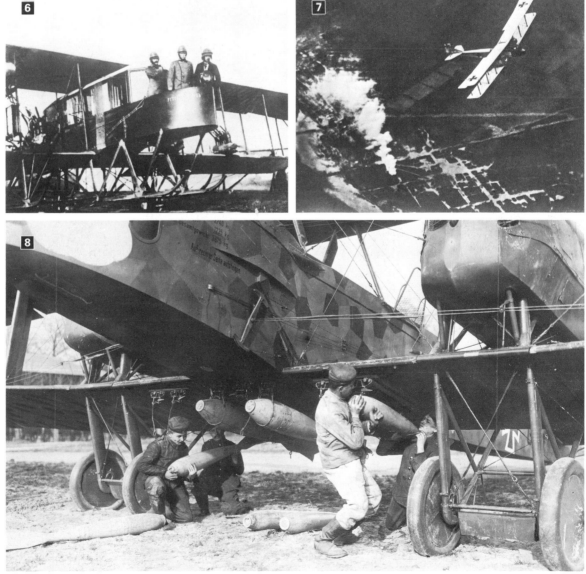

Naval aviation

1 The Royal Naval Air Service came into being on 23 June 1914 and quickly established itself as a progressive force, ready to experiment with the possibilities offered by naval aviation. Here a Sopwith Pup makes the first successful landing at sea, on the aircraft carrier HMS *Furious* in 1917. The rope framework was intended to act as a safety barrier.

2 After the first landing the Pup's pilot, Squadron Commander Dunning, decided on a second attempt. This was a fatal mistake, as the aircraft landed badly and bounced off the deck, killing its pilot. The photograph shows the helpless deck crew trying to stop the Pup going over the side.

3 An aerial view of the carrier *Furious*, a modern-looking design that foreshadowed the massive 'flat tops' of World War II.

4 A two-seater Short Seaplane 184 flies over coastal waters while on a reconnaissance patrol. The 240hp Sunbeam engine provided the aircraft with a maximum speed of 124km/h (77mph). The development of the U-boat threat to British shipping gave the 184 a new role of submarine-spotter. To avoid detection the U-boats were forced to travel submerged in coastal waters, reducing their speed and range drastically.

5 One of the more innovative weapon developments of the war: a Sopwith Baby seaplane fires Le Prieur rockets, designed to shoot down balloons whose gas-filled interiors were vulnerable to rockets and other incendiary projectiles. The Sopwith Baby was a versatile naval aircraft and besides the rockets its range of armaments included two 30kg (65lb) bombs, Ranken darts (for use against U-boats), and a Lewis machine gun. It operated in the North Sea and the Mediterranean throughout the war, flying bombing, reconnaissance, anti-submarine and anti-Zeppelin missions.

6 The torpedo proved itself to be a formidable weapon during the war and with the development of sufficiently powerful aircraft it was only logical that they should be torpedo-armed. This Sunbeam Cuckoo is in the act of releasing its torpedo.

7 A Sopwith Camel awaits its launch from a short platform built over the 'B' turret of the battlecruiser HMS *Repulse*. By 1917 flying-off platforms were being introduced on the Royal Navy's major warships as a quick means of supplying aerial reconnaissance. However, there were no facilities for landing, and if a shore-based airfield was not within the range of the aircraft, it had to ditch in the sea.

Chapter 9 The Eastern Front 1916-18

Above: Alexander Kerensky, Minister of War in the Russian Provisional Government, takes the salute during an army parade. Kerensky's determination to carry on the war against Germany led to the fall of his government at the hands of the Bolsheviks.

Below: V.I. Lenin, leader of the Bolshevik Party and mastermind of the October Revolution, appears in disguise.

The German Army had inflicted a massive and costly defeat on Russia in the great summer offensive of 1915, and as the German High Command turned its attention to the west in 1916 it hoped that Russia would remain on the defensive. The Russian Army, after 18 months of fighting, remained a cumbersome military machine led, in the main, by ill-educated generals with old-fashioned ideas about the conduct of war. By 1916, however, there was some cause for optimism as Russia's industrial resources at last began to expand. The chronic shortages of weapons, ammunition and other essential items of military equipment which had undermined Russian efforts in 1914–15 had been overcome by the spring of 1916. Conforming to the plans agreed between the Allies, the Russian High Command made preparations for renewed offensives on the Eastern Front.

At a major planning conference on 14 April 1916 attended by the Tsar and his army group commanders, it was agreed to adopt an unorthodox offensive scheme put forward by General Alexei Brusilov, commanding the Southwest Army Group. His plan consisted of a wide-fronted advance, making maximum use of the element of surprise. Brusilov was one of the few Russian commanders at ease with the latest advances in military technology. Aerial photography, the construction of offensive trench systems, concealment of reserves and good artillery–infantry co-operation all played a part in his preparations for the coming offensive.

On 4 June the four armies of Brusilov's Group (38 divisions against an Austro-German force of similar strength) attacked along a dispersed front of over 300km (190 miles). The Russians' careful preparations and tight pre-offensive security paid off, and the surprised Austro-Hungarian forces fell back in disarray. The Russians pressed forward quickly: an advance of 80km (50 miles) by 12 June netted nearly 200,000 Austrian prisoners and vast stores of enemy equipment. At this point support from his neighbours and strong reinforcements were needed, but despite Brusilov's entreaties for prompt action the response was slow. Yet again German reinforcements arrived just in time to shore up a collapsing Austrian front. After a period of reorganisation, Brusilov's offensive was resumed in late July and August; by the beginning of September the Austrians had lost over 600,000 men and the Germans 150,000. Fighting continued during September (the peak of the Battle of the Somme) but as Russian casualties mounted, the forward impetus of the advance could not be maintained, and it slowly ground to a halt.

The Brusilov offensive was a near-fatal blow to the Austro-Hungarian Empire. It also forced the German High Command to withdraw divisions from the Somme front in the west. And it produced a new enemy of the Central Powers in the east. Encouraged by Allied promises of territory from Austria-Hungary and by the Russian success under Brusilov, Romania declared war on 27 August against Austria-Hungary. This proved to be a fatal military error: Romania's army of 23 divisions was obsolete by 1916 standards, and surrounded by enemies, her strategic position was extremely vulnerable.

General von Falkenhayn was dismissed as German Chief-of-Staff on 28 August and at once appointed commander of the combined Austro-German-Bulgarian operation against Romania. He himself took direct command of the Austro-German forces to the north. Bucharest fell on 6 December to a combined thrust by General August von Mackensen from the south and von Falkenhayn, driving the remnants of the Romanian Army northeast to the protection of Russian forces in Moldavia. For minimal casualties the Germans now controlled most of Romania, ruthlessly exploiting the country's important economic resources of oil and grain for the benefit of a blockaded Germany.

The fall of Romania led to an extension of the Russian line down to the Black Sea and a further drain on her manpower reserves. By the end of 1916 her total casualties were estimated at around 5,000,000. Shortages of foodstuffs during the bitter winter of 1916–17 led to riots in the big cities, and a growing revolutionary mood. In March 1917, against a background of mass demonstrations and the breakdown of discipline in the police and army, Tsar Nicholas II was deposed, and a Provisional Government was set up. The new government, basically liberal in character, was committed to the continuation of the war and was at first expected to strengthen Russia's war effort. However, its authority was increasingly undermined by the activities of left-wing groups whose demands for

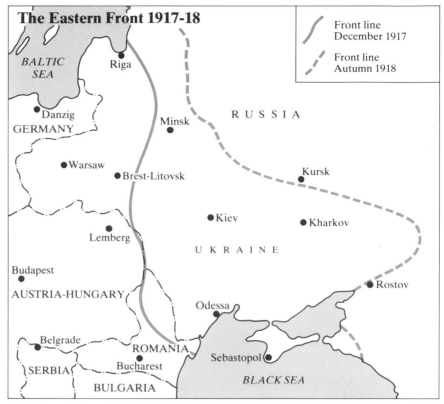

The Eastern Front 1917-18

Front line December 1917

Front line Autumn 1918

'peace and bread' met with a ready response from the war-weary Russian peasants and soldiers.

War-weariness, by 1917, was not confined to Russia. Italy, in just over a year and a half of war, had suffered losses of about 750,000, and the mood of patriotic excitement with which she had entered the war was dying away. In France, as well as the army mutinies, there was demoralisation on the home front as a series of traitorous scandals affecting members of the government came to light. In Britain, the shock of conscription was added to the equal shocks of air bombardment and food shortages due to submarine blockade. The International Socialist Conference in Stockholm in June provided a focus for discontent, but Russia's example was the most important stimulus to action.

Despite growing disaffection within the army, the Minister of War, A.F. Kerensky, determined upon renewed offensive action to rekindle Russian patriotism. This took the shape of an attack in Galicia (the Kerensky offensive) on 1 July 1917. Some progress was made during the first week of fighting but a crushing counter-offensive brought the Russian advance to a dead halt. The Russian soldiers had had enough and now retreated in vast numbers. In Lenin's words 'they voted for peace with their legs'; from August onwards the army disintegrated, mutinies and mass desertions becoming commonplace. In September the Germans followed up their repulse of Kerensky's attack with a limited offensive of their own, the capture of the Baltic port of Riga by von Hutier's Eighth Army. The attack was notable for the first use of the tactic of 'predicted shooting', devised by Colonel Bruchmüller. This technique restored the long-lost element of surprise, permitting a German advance of nearly 16km (10 miles) on the first day.

The weakness of the Russian Provisional Government enabled the Bolshevik faction of the Social Democrats to seize power in November 1917 (the famous 'October Revolution' – so-called because of

Russia's adherence to the old Julian calendar, 13 days behind the international system). Under the determined leadership of Lenin and Trotsky, the Bolsheviks had little trouble ousting the government and once in power immediately sought peace. The German High Command saw in this a marvellous opportunity, first to seize large areas of Russia, and secondly, to transfer the bulk of the German Army in the east to the Western Front. On 15 December 1917 an armistice agreement was signed at Brest-Litovsk, to be followed by peace negotiations in the New Year.

As negotiations between the German and Bolshevik representatives began, German forces moved deep into the Ukraine (whose newly formed government owed its existence to German 'patronage'), and despite the armistice invaded Russian territory from the Baltic to the Black Sea. The Bolsheviks had no means with which to oppose the Central Powers and the victors' terms for a peace settlement were harsh in the extreme. Faced with civil war and ruthless invasion, the Bolsheviks were forced to accept; the Treaty of Brest-Litovsk was signed on 3 March 1918. By its terms Russia lost 34 per cent of her population and some of her most productive areas containing 54 per cent of her industry.

Despite the decision of the German High Command that the war would be decided in the west, the new opportunities for expansion in the east deflected them from their original aim. Large numbers of German troops remained in the east and continued to advance into southern Russia. The Crimea was occupied in April 1918 (in total violation of the Brest-Litovsk Treaty) and a few weeks later the Germans had secured control of Rostov and the economically important Donetz basin. In the north, German units moved into Finland, and plans were drawn up for the seizure of Petrograd and the overthrow of the Bolshevik regime. Only the defeat of Germany on the Western Front woke her from her dream of expansion in the east.

Above left: General Alexei Brusilov, one of the most talented commanders to emerge from World War I. His offensive in the summer of 1916 demonstrated a complete mastery of the techniques of modern war.

Above: The Bolshevik withdrawal from the war did not bring an end to the fighting on the Eastern Front. While civil war broke out between the rival political factions within Russia, the Germans cynically disregarded the terms of the Treaty of Brest-Litovsk, and sent their forces deep into southern Russia.

The Eastern Front 1916

1 Their heads bowed forward, as if walking through a heavy rainstorm, Russian troops pick their way through a barbed-wire entanglement under heavy smallarms fire during the initial stages of the Brusilov offensive. The offensive opened on 4 June after a one-day bombardment.

2 Russian artillerymen fuze the shells for their 76.2mm field gun during close-range fighting on the edge of a wood. In 1916 the front-line troops began to receive adequate stocks of ammunition for the first time, as a consequence of Russian industry placing itself on a war footing. Thus, for example, the manufacture of shells rose from 358,000 a month in January 1915 to 1,512,000 by November and then to a peak of 2,900,000 in September 1916.

3 This 7.62mm PM1910 machine gun of the Russian Army has a rather unusual mount, consisting of both an extended tripod and wheels with a protective shield.

4 Gas remained a feature of warfare on the Eastern Front, and the rank-and-file of this Austrian rifle section have already donned their masks in expectation of an attack.

5 Looking like pantomime ghosts, this group of Russian infantrymen are posing for the camera wearing the Russian-style gas mask.

6 Russian troops relax in a carefully dug entrenchment with wattle revetments on the Eastern Front. Whereas in the West the front line consisted of a near-continuous series of trenches, the vast distances of the Eastern Front prevented this development, and only key points were protected by trench fortifications.

7 Russian dead lie where they fell during one of many battles that made up the Brusilov offensive. Austria-Hungary was never to recover from this hammer blow in the East, but Russian casualties were also massive, and by the end of 1916 had reached a horrifying total for the whole war of around 5,000,000.

Destruction of Romania

1 A Romanian cavalryman, armed with the traditional weapon of the horseman, the lance, and a more modern rifle-carbine.

2 Romanian troops cross a makeshift bridge, withdrawing from the onslaught of the German armies. Romania's decision to join the war on the side of the Allies was one of the great misjudgements of the war. Inspired by the success of the Brusilov offensive, the Romanians declared war on Austria on 27 August 1916, but by then the Russian advance was slowing up and Romania was isolated.

3 Wearing parade uniforms, a detachment of Romanian infantry proudly marches through the capital of Bucharest on the day war is declared.

4 Although Romanian troops made a few hesitant probes over the Transylvanian and Carpathian Mountains in September 1916, the arrival of the German Ninth Army soon threw them back on the defensive. Here a German 21cm howitzer is made ready in a gun-pit in Romania. The poorly equipped Romanian armies had no answer to such well-handled firepower.

5 Billowing black clouds rise from an oil dump near the coastal town of Constanza.

6 A street scene in Bucharest after its capture by the Germans on 6 December 1916. Despite losing their capital the Romanians conducted a fighting retreat northwards towards Moldavia and the Russian border. There they were reinforced by the Russians, and they clung on to northeast Romania for the remainder of the war.

7 A column of Austrian troops marches through a main street in Romania. The Austrians had played a very minor part in the offensive, but like Bulgaria and Turkey they too wanted a slice of the cake. Germany paid little heed to the squabbles and demands of its minor allies; it held the power in Romania and the country's oil and wheat went north to Germany.

Defeat and desertion
Collapse of the Russian Army

1 Upturned rifles mark the spot where these Russian soldiers met their death, victims of the German offensive against Riga in September 1917.

2 The fall of the Tsar and his government had led to the appointment of a Provisional Government under the leadership of Kerensky. While the Provisional Government kept Russia in the war, the emerging Bolshevik Party campaigned for an immediate end to hostilities. The war-weary Russian soldiery were a sympathetic audience for the Bolshevik agitators who toured the country gaining support for their proposals. Here a Bolshevik orator stands amid his supporters in the naval base of Kronstadt – famed for its Bolshevik leanings.

3 After the failure of Kerensky's offensive in Galicia in July 1917, the exhausted Russian Army began to disintegrate. The Provisional Government's hopes for a military solution to the war came to nothing as Russian soldiers began deserting in droves.

4 Troops from a Russian infantry battalion take to their heels after hearing reports that they are about to be attacked by German cavalry. The original British caption notes with disapproval the influence of the Bolsheviks. While the Western nations had little sympathy with the Tsarist regime, they were horrified by Bolshevik threats to pull Russia out of the war.

5 The revolution of November 1917 (October in the old calendar) brought the Bolsheviks to power with comparative ease. On 17 December an armistice with Germany came into effect, and the two sides met at Brest-Litovsk to discuss peace terms. Here the Russian delegation is met off the train by its German counterparts. Leader of the Russian team, Leon Trotsky, stands centre right, with fur cap and dark coat.

6 German and Russian delegates at the peace negotiations in Brest-Litovsk. The Germans forced rapacious demands on a defenceless Russia.

The October Revolution

1 Rifle-fire sends demonstrators scattering along Nevski Prospect in Petrograd (St Petersburg). The period between the first 'February' Revolution (March 1917) and the Bolshevik 'October' Revolution (November 1917) was one of political confusion as the Provisional Government attempted the impossible dual task of keeping power and fighting the war. Assailed from both left and right, the Provisional Government had only a tenuous hold on affairs, and as popular support drained away it became ripe for overthrow.

2 Soldiers and sailors in Petrograd avidly read a news-sheet issued by the government. A hard-fought propaganda war was waged by the differing parties for the support of the masses. In this the Bolsheviks were past masters.

3 Tsar Nicholas II (centre) before his deposition, with his son and heir, dressed up in ceremonial cossack uniforms. Already an embarrassment to the Provisional Government, the arrival of the Red Bolsheviks in power turned the Russian royal family into a rallying-point for the anti-communist White forces. As Russia degenerated into civil war, therefore, the royal family was killed.

4/5 Bolshevik soldiers patrol the streets of Petrograd during the winter of 1917–18, with the revolution far from secure.

6 Red soldiers celebrate the Bolshevik revolution. The seizure of power was masterminded by Lenin and Trotsky and the well-organised Bolsheviks had little trouble overthrowing the crumbling edifice of the Provisional Government.

The war in Russia 1918
Germany invades

1 A German field howitzer fires on Russian positions, August 1917.

2 Anti-Bolshevik White Russian troops crossing a river in southern Russia, September 1918.

3 After the ceasefire of December 1917 German troops were encouraged to fraternise with their former enemy, to further the dissolution of the Russian Army. However, this led to German troops picking up the 'virus' of Bolshevism.

4 A White Russian bomber squadron assembles its French-built Voisin aircraft at an airfield near Rostov. Both the Germans and the Allies gave aid to the anti-Bolshevik forces.

5 The Kaiser (far left) talks with the Hetman of the Ukraine, September 1918. As part of their policy of dismembering the Russian Empire, the Germans set up vassal states along the Baltic and in the Ukraine.

6 German infantry set off in pursuit of Bolshevik partisans, in the winter of 1917–18. Germany cynically disregarded the terms of the Treaty of Brest-Litovsk and in 1918 continued its advance into Russia. Some 40 divisions were kept in Russia during Germany's great gamble in the West.

7 German troops shelter behind a 7.7cm field gun in an engagement with Bolshevik forces.

Fighting for a homeland
The Polish and Czech Legions

1 Polish troops fighting with the Austro-Hungarian Army fire upon a Russian-occupied village in Galicia, December 1914.

2 The appointment of the Polish Regency Council in Warsaw, 15 October 1917. This was Austria's attempt to set up a dependent state out of the old Russian-controlled Polish province.

3 Wearing their traditional square-topped *Czapka* helmets, cavalrymen of the Polish Legion prepare for action. The Austrians encouraged the Poles to fight for them against the Russians with various promises of sovereignty after the war.

4 Polish troops in France parade in a village square.

5 A Czech armoured train on the Trans-Siberian railway, near Omsk, May 1918. Of all the nations of the Austro-Hungarian Empire the Czechs were the most organised in their opposition to rule from Vienna. Large numbers of Czechs surrendered to the Russians during the war, and upon being freed after the revolution they formed the Czech Legion to fight for the formation of a national state.

6 The newly freed Czechs found themselves confronted by a highly confused political situation in Russia. After seizing an armoured train from the Bolsheviks they proceeded to fight their way eastward along the Trans-Siberian Railway. These men are guarding a train in temperatures of 40 degrees below freezing.

7 Nationalist leader T.G. Masaryk triumphantly enters Prague on 21 December 1918 to assume the presidency of the newly created republic.

8 Czech soldiers skirmish with Bolshevik troops on the outskirts of Ekaterinburg in the early spring of 1918.

Chapter 10 Decision in the West

Above: Commander-in-Chief of the US Army in France, General John Pershing maintained an iron control over the autonomy of his army.

Below: Germany's war leaders: the Kaiser is flanked by von Hindenburg (left) and Ludendorff at German Army Headquarters.

By the beginning of 1918, all the Allied armies were suffering from serious manpower shortages. French reserves were exhausted, and it was only with difficulty that 99 divisions were maintained on the Western Front. Italy was still reeling from the Caporetto disaster. Five British divisions (over 100,000 men) had been sent to the Italian front, while at the same time strong forces were preparing a new offensive against the Turks in Palestine. Meanwhile the government had decreed a reorganisation of the BEF which meant a reduction of 141 battalions although its front was simultaneously extended by some 40km (25 miles).

Germany, by now, was virtually a military dictatorship, ruled by Hindenburg and Ludendorff. They recognised that, despite the obvious weaknesses of the Allies, Germany's military position was dangerous. The heavy fighting of 1917 had gravely weakened the army and lowered its efficiency and morale. The U-boat campaign, which had been expected to decide the issue after a few months, had clearly failed to do so. Germany herself was now suffering badly from the rigours of blockade. And although few American troops were yet in the battle line, their numbers were steadily increasing, and would evidently offset the German forces being released from the Eastern Front. It was a position that could only get worse, and the High Command now decided upon a gambler's throw aimed at defeating the Allies outright: a spring offensive against the British armies on the Somme–Arras front.

The German strength on the Western Front rose steadily during the early months of 1918, but the High Command did not rely solely on numbers. All through 1917 the Germans had developed their infiltration tactics, forming units of specialised 'Storm Troops' to put them into operation. The new tactics and the elite troops were used for the first time in the counter-attack at Cambrai on 30 November 1917, and their success was striking. In addition, the massive German artillery component planned to use the technique of predicted shooting which had been so successful at Riga – once more orchestrated by Colonel Bruchmüller. During February and March 1918 preparations were made for the coming offensive. German staff-work was excellent; guns, ammunition, supplies and vast numbers of men were brought forward with the utmost secrecy.

Codenamed Operation Michael, the German offensive was carried out by the Seventeenth Army (von Below), Second Army (von der Marwitz) and Eighteenth Army (von Hutier), totalling 59 divisions, and supported by the largest concentration of artillery that had ever been assembled: 6473 guns and howitzers and 3532 trench mortars. Along a front of 80km (50 miles) the Germans were faced with the 12 infantry divisions of the British Fifth Army (Gough) and further to the north, General Byng's Third Army of 14 divisions. The Fifth Army had just taken over a section of the French line and had still not completed its defences when Operation Michael was launched. The staff of the Fifth Army had accurately predicted the German attack, but Gough's army was weak in relation to the length of front held and there were very few reserves behind it.

The massed German guns opened the great offensive with a shattering five-hour bombardment at 0510 hours on 21 March 1918. A thick morning mist proved invaluable to the attacking Storm Troops, and the badly battered British front-line positions were overrun with comparative ease. By the end of the first day's fighting both the Fifth and Third Armies were in retreat. British casualties on 21 March were estimated at 38,512 (including 21,000 prisoners) but the Germans had suffered even greater losses. During the next week the British continued to retreat as Ludendorff exploited his initial success; by the end of March, 83 German divisions had been engaged in the battle.

As the German advance continued, a grave risk of separation faced the Allied armies. General Pétain feared a further attack on the French sector, and was reluctant to support the British. To overcome this, at Haig's instigation a unified command was set up on 26 March, when General Ferdinand Foch was appointed to coordinate all British and French forces. French units were then moved northward to aid the hard-pressed British.

By 28 March – having penetrated the British lines to a maximum depth of 65km (40 miles) – the German effort began to weaken. The Third Army repulsed an assault against Arras, while the key centre of Amiens remained just out of German reach. Having failed to break the British with the Michael offensive, a second blow (Operation George) was delivered further

The German Offensives of 1918

Front line
March 1918

Maximum limit
of German gains

Above right: The German offensives of 1918 were a desperate attempt to stave off defeat, and their failure revealed the bankruptcy of German strategy.

Above: Field Marshal Sir Douglas Haig. Vilified after the war as a commander who wasted men's lives, Haig was in fact the leading general of the Allied side. His strategy of wearing down the German Army was vindicated in the great battles of the summer and autumn of 1918.

north in Flanders along the River Lys. This continued until 30 April, and although the British forces had, in Haig's own words, their 'backs to the wall', once more the Germans failed to obtain their objective.

Flanders nevertheless continued to be Ludendorff's favoured theatre of operations; he realised, however, that before he attacked the British again he first had to force the withdrawal of French divisions (13 infantry and three cavalry) from the British sector. Accordingly, a heavy diversionary attack was planned on the *Chemin des Dames* in Champagne. Great secrecy surrounded the German preparations, which included the assembly of 4000 guns on a narrow front, once more under the direction of Bruchmüller. The attack (known as the Third Battle of the Aisne) began at 0100 hours on 27 May, taking the French command entirely by surprise. Its success surprised the Germans themselves – the first day saw the deepest single-day penetration on the Western Front of the whole war. By 3 June the Germans had once again reached the River Marne.

The German line now formed a huge bulge, inviting counter-attack. Their attempts to broaden it out met with little success, and the French, reinforced by British, American and even Italian divisions, prepared a counter-stroke. The last German offensive of the war was launched on 15 June, and immediately ground to a halt. On 18 June Foch struck back – the Second Battle of the Marne – a victory which marked the passing of the strategic initiative to the Allies at last.

More immediately, it marked the end of any possibility of another German attack on the British in Flanders. Instead, the BEF itself prepared for a new offensive, which duly began on 8 August, a date which

Ludendorff called 'the black day of the German Army'. On that day the Australians, Canadians and British troops of General Rawlinson's Fourth Army, with a French army attacking beside them, opened the Battle of Amiens. As at Cambrai in 1917, the initial success was obtained by a devastating bombardment by predicted shooting, and this was followed by the onset of 414 fighting tanks masked by a dense fog. By 11 August the issue of the battle was no longer in doubt; it was on that day that the Kaiser said, 'The war must be ended.'

Rawlinson's army was now approaching the shattered landscape of the 1916 Somme battlefields – a formidable obstacle. Haig was determined not to become bogged in this ill-omened area, and now steadily extended his front of attack northwards, bringing in the Third Army (Byng) on 21 August (the Battle of Albert), and the First Army (Horne) on 26 August (the Battle of the Scarpe). The British advance was continuous; on their right the French attacked at Noyon, and on 12 September the Americans fought and won their first great battle at St Mihiel.

The climax of the whole Allied offensive came in late September, with the British attack on the Hindenburg Line, while the French and Americans opened a new offensive in the Argonne, and a mixed Belgian-British-French army group attacked in Flanders. On 29 September the British Fourth Army broke through the Hindenburg Line – a magnificent feat of arms which produced 35,000 prisoners and 380 captured guns. This was the beginning of the end. It was on this day that the German High Command concluded that the only thing to do was to make an immediate approach to President Woodrow Wilson, requesting his good offices for an armistice and peace.

Germany's home front

1 A run on a German savings bank in Berlin at the outbreak of war, 1 August 1914. Inevitably the war disrupted the workings of international finance, but stability was maintained with governmental assurances.

2 Raising money to finance the war: wealthy, patriotic Germans pay for the privilege of driving nails into an Iron Cross. Enthusiasm for the war in 1914 came from all sections of society, crossing class barriers and transcending differences of political affiliation.

3 The wounded were highly regarded and until the latter stages of the war, were well-treated by the Fatherland. Here convalescent troops are taken out on a sightseeing tour.

4 Front-line inspection: as part of a fund-raising drive German civilians are shown round a dummy trench system in a Berlin park.

5 The harsh realities of war are revealed in this (highly posed) photograph of a despairing mother with her two children, the newly opened letter informing her of the death of her husband at the front. The directors of the war – the Kaiser flanked by von Hindenburg and Ludendorff – look down from a photograph on the wall. The effect of the Royal Navy's blockade caused severe shortages for the Central Powers, but only after the harsh 'Turnip Winter' of 1916–17 (when turnips replaced potatoes) were essential foodstuffs in short supply. By 1918 starvation was a stark fact for the poor in Germany.

6 Manpower shortages forced German manufacturers to look elsewhere for labour. Here German women prepare shell casings in an arms factory.

7 Air-raid damage to a railway station at Diederhofen, 18 January 1918. The Independent Air Force dropped 328 tonnes of bombs on civilian targets during the war, causing alarm out of all proportion to damage and casualties.

Operation Michael
Germany's great gamble

1 A German gun-crew loads a 15cm howitzer. Under the guidance of Germany's leading artillery tactician, Colonel Bruchmüller, the artillery preparations for Operation Michael were the greatest yet seen. Some 6473 guns and 3532 trench mortars were secretly assembled and hidden along the front. The attack opened on 21 March 1918 with a massive bombardment.

2 Gas projectors being prepared for action. Gas was an integral part of Bruchmüller's plans, forcing the British into gas masks which slowed movement and dulled responses.

3 German Storm Troops are instructed in infiltration tactics at the great training camp at Sedan. To minimise casualties and keep the advance moving, the Storm Troops were taught to bypass strongpoints and push forward to overrun the enemy as quickly as possible. The Germans assembled three armies, comprising 74 divisions (around a million men) for the offensive. Nothing was left to chance.

4 Long-range heavy firepower was provided by weapons such as this 40cm railway gun, aimed at Allied positions far behind the front line.

5 German troops race out of shell craters to assault enemy positions following the discharge of a trench mortar. Artillery and Storm Troop units were trained in close-cooperation techniques.

6 German infantry and artillery crowding together in the wrecked streets of St Quentin on the first day of the great attack, 21 March 1918. Keeping the momentum going with such vast numbers of men, weapons and equipment was a major logistical achievement, and a credit to the work of the staff officers.

Retreat and recovery
The British Army holds the line

1 The German bombardment caused havoc in the British lines, and oncoming German troops were greeted by sights such as these, slain defenders guarding flattened trenches.

2 A British 60-pounder, firing in open country, in an attempt to slow the German attackers. Many guns were lost through the speed of the German advance. A total of 532 guns were captured on the first day – the highest loss in British military history.

3 For the first time since the Battle of Mons British troops were in retreat. Here infantry-men march through the village of Aveluy, past the MkIV tanks of the 2nd Battalion, the Tank Corps. The retreat was carried out in good order for the most part, and panic was rare.

4 French and British troops dig in against an expected German attack. The German penetration was such that they passed through the British trench lines to the open country beyond; the first signs of a return to a war of movement. Being short of reserves to patch the great hole made in the British Fifth Army's line, Field Marshal Haig appealed to the French for help. Fearful of a major attack on his own sector, however, Marshal Pétain was slow in sending forces.

5 New Zealand infantry march past Whippet tanks of the 3rd Battalion at Mailly-Maillet, 26 March. This day was the debut of the Whippet tank in action. The German offensive caught the Tank Corps reorganising its forces, however, and they played only a limited role in defending the line.

6 The blind leading the blind: British gas casualties wait for attention at an advanced dressing station. British casualties on 21 March 1918 were only exceeded by those incurred on 1 July 1916 (the first day of the Somme) and were estimated to be in the region of 38,500 men, including 21,000 prisoners. More significant, however, were the losses sustained by the Germans, of nearly 40,000 men. German progress began to falter in the face of stiffening British resistance, and when the German troops discovered the Allied food supplies, they stopped to loot with increasing degrees of indiscipline.

Second Battle of the Marne
The French under fire

1 German infantry dash through a cut barbed-wire entanglement on the Aisne. Ludendorff's offensive against the French (launched on 27 May) was intended as a diversionary operation but the initial success of the attack led the Germans to develop the battle further, thereby using up valuable reserves.

2 A German field-gun battery in action during the offensive. The German artillery bombardment that opened the attack was even more intense than that of Operation Michael. All resistance was crushed and the infantry had an easier task than usual – merely to take possession of the battered front-line positions.

3 German troops march towards the front. As the German salient got bigger so more and more men were needed just to hold the line. Germany used up her best troops in these offensives.

4 A St Chamond tank crosses a front-line trench to lead a French counter-attack against the Germans. By early June the balance of strength was beginning to pass to the French, and on 18 June General Mangin's Tenth Army launched a major counter-offensive which began to force the Germans back out of the salient. The strategic initiative had reverted to the Allies.

5 German transport drivers and horses wear gas masks during the advance on Soissons, June 1918. Although motor tractors were becoming more common, horses remained the most usual prime mover on the battlefield.

6 A German machine-gun crew fires upon enemy positions near the Marne.

7 British and French troops prepare for a German attack on the third day of the offensive, 29 May. Five battered British divisions had been sent south to recuperate in this customarily quiet sector after the battles in Picardy and Flanders. They received the main brunt of the German attack, however.

Haig's offensive
Battle of Amiens

1 The quality of British artillery improved steadily throughout the war so that by the summer of 1918 it had gained an ascendancy over its German opposite numbers. Before the Battle of Amiens the position of German batteries had been carefully pinpointed and as soon as the main barrage opened up they were overwhelmed by a hurricane of British fire. There was little German counter-battery fire. This German gun was caught up in the battle on 8 August 1918 and hit by British artillery fire before it could unlimber.

2 The Australian and Canadian Corps acted as a spearhead for the British advance and their own corps artillery worked to good effect in supporting the infantry advance. Here Australian gunners stand beside their 4.5in field howitzers during a pause in the fighting. Light in weight and yet firing a reasonably heavy shell of 15.9kg (35lb), the 4.5in howitzer had a range of 6675m (7300yd) – this was somewhat short by the standards of 1918, however.

3 Beside the barbed wire of a German position near Sailly Laurette, British troops of the III Corps examine a captured German 08/15 light machine gun. The III Corps, unlike its fellow Dominion Corps, failed to make much headway in the first day's fighting, but subsequently did better in securing its objectives.

4 MkV tanks trundle past British and Dominion troops. The trenches of the previous year have given way to open countryside.

5 Some of the 30,000 Germans captured at Amiens march back to a prisoner-of-war cage. The British victory at Amiens was one of the great triumphs of the war and its strategic effects were far-reaching, Ludendorff called 8 August the 'black day of the German Army' and it convinced the German High Command that the war was lost.

Breaching the Hindenburg Line

1 British armoured cars set out on a reconnaissance mission in the Somme region. Now that manoeuvre had returned to war, mobility regained its importance.

2 The crossing of the St Quentin Canal by men of the 46th Division, 29 September 1918. Their passage of the canal near Bellenglise was a superb feat of arms: the steep-sided canal was crossed in the face of heavy machine-gun fire, and yet by dusk the division had advanced a further 5km (3 miles) and captured 4200 prisoners for a loss of 800 men.

3 British infantry scramble across the Canal du Nord. The Hindenburg Line was breached after a ferocious bombardment by British artillery: from noon on 28 September to noon on 29 September 943,847 rounds were fired, the highest British 24-hour total of the war.

4 MkV tanks move forward with 'cribs' to aid their crossing of the Hindenburg Line near Bellicourt, September 1918.

5 The liberation of Lille: British troops are greeted by French children after four years of occupation.

6 Some of the 188,700 prisoners captured by the British Army during the battles of 1918. The British contribution to the defeat of Germany on the Western Front was decisive.

Communications

1 Royal Field Artillery signallers flash back news of the capture of Chipilly Ridge by the 58th Division in the Battle of Amiens, 9 August 1918. The telescope is for receiving signals while the heliograph (far right) sends them.

2 In the middle of a gas attack a soldier of the Army Signal Service taps out a message on a 'fullerphone' scrambler.

3 High in the Argonne German signallers prepare to transmit a message by means of a gas-operated arc light.

4 A German military telephone exchange in operation. As radio communication was still in its infancy, the armies of World War I were forced to rely on the telephone – with all its inadequacies.

5 An attempt to make the telephone mobile: a German field telephone on the edge of no man's land.

6 Even as late as 1918, recourse was made to primitive forms of communication, such as this homing pigeon about to be released from a British tank during the Battle of Amiens.

7 Another form of animal signal: a Royal Engineer reads a dog-borne message, the messenger wet from his canal crossing.

The Americans in action

1 Fighting from improvised defences, an American infantryman fires his 7.7mm Chauchat light machine gun. His Number Two has one of the gun's distinctive magazines at hand – as instructed in the drill book. The Americans showed their fighting spirit at the Battle of Cantigny on 28 May 1918, and achieved lasting fame for their dogged battle at Belleau Wood from 4 June to 10 July.

2 As part of their preparation for trench warfare units of the US Army would often take over a quiet sector of the front. These troops are holding a trench on a wooded hillside in the Vosges Mountains. The first major US action of the war was the eradication of the St Mihiel Salient on 12–13 September 1918, which involved over 200,000 men.

3 Sitting on top of French-built Renault FT17 light tanks, US troops move up to the wooded hills of the Argonne, 26 September 1918. After the victory at St Mihiel, Pershing and his fellow American commanders expected great things from the First Army, which was to operate alongside the French Fourth in a general assault. The terrrain favoured defensive operations, however, and inexperienced US officers lacked the ability to coordinate an all-arms battle. Poor logistics caused further confusion, and faced with skilful German counter-attacks Pershing was forced to call a halt.

4 US troops train with phosphorus rifle grenades, a new and fearsome anti-personnel weapon in the American armoury.

5 A US-manned tank behind them, American infantrymen prepare to advance from hastily dug 'scrapes'.

6 A temporary respite from the horrors of war: American troops amuse themselves at the piano in a ruined church. Although the war ended before the full potential of the US Army could be realised, it nonetheless made a spirited contribution to the overall Allied victory.

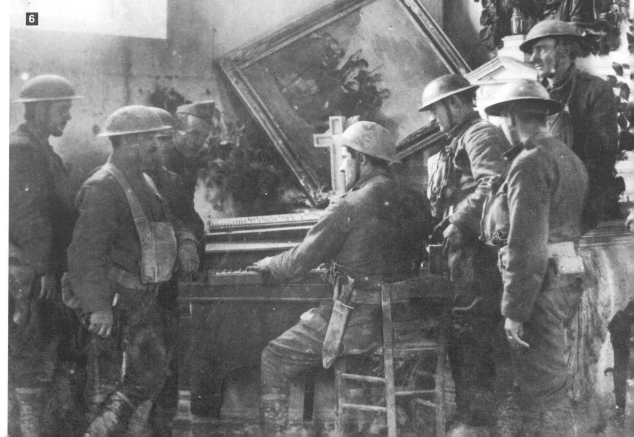

Chapter 11 Defeat of the Central Powers

Above: Marshal Foch assumed supreme command on the Western Front at the height of the Michael offensive on 26 March, in order to coordinate the various efforts of the Allied armies. An inspirational leader, Foch gained the respect of all the Allied Commanders-in-Chief through his tactful handling of the many crises of 1918 and his determination to defeat the Germans.

Below right: General Sir Edmund Allenby decisively defeated the Turks at Megiddo in September 1918 and brought the campaign in Palestine to a victorious conclusion for the British.

Opposite page, above: General Sir Henry Wilson, the British Chief of the Imperial General Staff during the last year of the war.

Opposite page, below: Turkey and her neighbouring ally Bulgaria were knocked out of the war by Allied successes in Mesopotamia, Palestine and the Balkans.

From the very first, Germany's allies were almost as much a liability as a help to her. All leaned heavily on German weaponry and munitions, on German expertise, and on German forces fighting on their various fronts. Their value to Germany was solely in their diversionary capability: the Austro-Hungarians against Russia, the Turks against Britain, and the Bulgarians against the large Allied force locked up in Salonika. As the war continued, however, all three grew weaker and more dependent on German aid, which became more and more difficult to supply as Germany's own position deteriorated.

Turkey, having been almost continuously at war since 1911, and ruling over a large disaffected Arab population, was perhaps the weakest of all. Her last attempt to reach the Suez Canal, in July 1916, was easily repelled. By the end of that year the British forces from Egypt, under General Sir Archibald Murray, had reached the border of Palestine (building a railway and laying a water pipeline as they went). An attempt to advance further in March 1917 was checked at Gaza by a combination of British error and the stubborn defensive quality of the Turkish soldiers which had already been demonstrated at Gallipoli. Murray was recalled and replaced by General Sir Edmund Allenby.

The British War Cabinet was anxious to obtain the propaganda victory of capturing Jerusalem before Christmas; Allenby was accordingly given powerful reinforcements which had been withheld from Murray. Allenby made no mistake when he launched his offensive in October; Gaza was taken on 7 November, and Jerusalem on 9 December. Turkey, simultaneously facing a widespread Arab revolt much inspired by Colonel T.E. Lawrence, and hard-hit by a British advance in Mesopotamia, was now in desperate straits.

These successes were bought at a price: the disproportionate diversion of British forces from the main front, where the Germans were about to launch their decisive stroke of 1918. When this occurred, in March/April, it became essential to call back British troops from the Middle East, thus putting a stop to offensive operations. However, the use of large numbers of Indian troops in both the Palestine and Mesopotamia armies made it possible to renew the offensive in September, with the Battle of Megiddo. This was a complete victory for Allenby, who made good use of his large contingent of cavalry as well as his small number of aircraft. The Turks were routed and their army now broke up; the Arabs entered Damascus on 1 October, Aleppo was captured on 26 October. In this sustained offensive and pursuit, Allenby had taken 75,000 prisoners at a cost of 5600 casualties – an indication of the utter collapse of a once-determined enemy.

It was the same in Mesopotamia. After their surrender at Kut in April 1916 the British adopted a defensive policy and concentrated on improving their rail and river communications. Reinforcements of Indian troops were brought in and heavy artillery accumulated. These enabled the new Commander-in-Chief, General Sir Stanley Maude, to begin an advance up

the Tigris in December; on 24 February 1917 the British re-entered Kut, and on 11 March they took Baghdad. There followed a lengthy pause during the hot season for consolidation, but Maude resumed his advance in September against a very weak enemy deprived of reinforcements by Allenby's threat in Palestine. On 18 November, in the midst of his skilful operations, General Maude died of cholera and was succeeded by Lieutenant-General Sir William Marshall, under whom the advance continued until the advent of the next hot season in March 1918.

Meanwhile, the cataclysmic events in Russia – the fall of the empire and the start of a civil war in 1918 – gave the Mesopotamian theatre a new, if modest, importance. Under Major-General Dunsterville an expedition known as 'Dunsterforce' was dispatched from Baghdad to cooperate with 'White' Russian troops on the Caspian Sea and to protect the oilfields around Baku from a threatened German-Turkish invasion. In September this force had to be withdrawn; the British campaign in Mesopotamia ended shortly afterwards when the Turkish Tigris Army surrendered. The Turks had fought resolutely against the British until the end, but the constant pressure of the campaigns in Palestine and Mesopotamia was too much for them. Furthermore, the collapse of Bulgaria at the end of September 1918 exposed Constantinople (Istanbul) to an Allied advance from Salonika, forcing Turkey to sue for peace. Turkish representatives met those of the Allies and on 30 October 1918 the Armistice of Mudros was signed, thereby ending hostilities.

The Allied forces in Salonika made a surprising resurgence in the autumn of 1918. The universally disliked French Commander-in-Chief, General Maurice Sarrail, had gone, and in July 1918 the dynamic

General Franchet d'Esperey took command of a force now comprising French, British, Italians, Serbs and Greeks. He immediately began planning a major offensive into occupied Serbia and Bulgaria. Although the Bulgarians had fought hard on the defensive along the border regions, by the summer of 1918 war-weariness was seriously undermining their morale, and German aid was no longer forthcoming. Franchet d'Esperey launched his final attack on 1 September. The Serbs enthusiastically forced their way over the mountain passes of Macedonia into their homeland. Bulgarian resistance collapsed under the combined thrusts of French, Serbian and British forces, and on 29 September an armistice was signed. This enabled the Allies to threaten Turkey and advance northward in October against the Austro-German armies in Romania and Hungary.

By 1918 Austria-Hungary's position was hopeless: politically the increasing momentum of Slav nationalism was tearing the empire apart, while on the military side German aid had practically ceased. On the Italian front, however, the Austrian Army remained an effective force. In June, it launched Austria's last offensive, a desperate attempt which was easily held by the Italian Army under the leadership of General Armando Diaz. The Italian Army had been substantially reorganised in the year since the Caporetto débâcle and on 24 October it went over to the offensive. The Austrian defences along the River Piave were breached, and the Austrian Army began a general retreat. The Italians followed (with French and British support) and won the final victory at Vittorio Veneto. On 27 October the Austrians sued for peace, and on 3 November an armistice brought the war on the Italian front to an end. This, in effect, signalled the demise of the Austro-Hungarian Empire.

Germany's end was not long delayed. The peace for which the High Command had clamoured when the Hindenburg Line was broken proved hard to obtain. Instead, there followed a month of continuous defeat and retreat in the west; the condition of the army became steadily more critical. On 26 October Ludendorff was dismissed, and replaced by General Wilhelm Gröner. Unrest was spreading through Germany, with demands for the Kaiser's abdication. On 29 October, mutiny broke out in the High Seas Fleet, and by 4 November Kiel had become a revolutionary centre flying the red flag. With the German Army now only scarcely able to fight but quite unable to move, the Allies launched their last offensive – the Americans again attacking in the Argonne, and the British on the Sambre. Between them the two Allied armies succeeded in taking 20,000 prisoners and 450 guns.

Revolution continued to spread; peace was now essential. On 7 November an armistice delegation crossed the lines; two days later the Kaiser abdicated and fled to Holland. A Republic was proclaimed, with the Social Democrat, Friedrich Ebert, as Chancellor. Imperial Germany was finished, but the generals of the Imperial Army had an alibi for their defeat – the legend of the 'stab in the back'. Yet the defeat was real enough: in the final three months the Allies had taken 385,400 prisoners and 6615 guns, of which the British share was just under 50 per cent of the prisoners and just over 40 per cent of the guns. The great catastrophe ended at 1100 hours on 11 November, when the armistice signed in Foch's specially fitted train came into effect, and the guns fell silent all along the line.

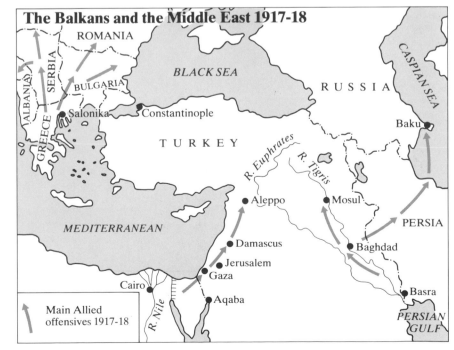

The Balkans and the Middle East 1917-18

ALBANIA · GREECE · SERBIA · ROMANIA · BULGARIA · Salonika · Constantinople · BLACK SEA · RUSSIA · CASPIAN SEA · Baku · TURKEY · R. Euphrates · R. Tigris · Mosul · PERSIA · Aleppo · Baghdad · MEDITERRANEAN · Damascus · Jerusalem · Gaza · Cairo · Aqaba · R. Nile · Basra · PERSIAN GULF

Main Allied offensives 1917-18

Desert adventure
Lawrence and the Arabs

1 Colonel T.E. Lawrence, British Army officer and desert legend. To the Arabs he was 'Al Auruns', a near-mystical figure who offered them a vision of Arab unity through victory over the Turks. A distinguished Arabist before the outbreak of war, Lawrence was posted to Cairo as an intelligence officer. When in June 1916 the Arabs of the Hejaz rose up against the Turks, Lawrence was sent into Arabia to report on the revolt. In collaboration with the Amir Feisal, Lawrence began the process of transforming the revolt into a full-scale guerrilla war.

2 Arab tribesmen at full charge on their camels. One of Lawrence's first tasks was to instil a degree of discipline into the unruly Arabs. Their concept of war was chivalric in inspiration; acts of individual bravery were everything, while the basic day-to-day details of military life were ignored as unworthy of serious consideration.

3 A keen photographer, Lawrence took this picture of Feisal's troops coming out of the desert, January 1917. The first phase of the campaign lasted from June 1916 to July 1917 and consisted of guerrilla raids against the Turkish railway running south to Medina.

4 A section of the railway is blown up near Deraa. Lawrence's policy was not to try and destroy the line to Medina, but rather by impeding its working to draw large numbers of Turkish troops to guard the railway. In the middle of 1917 Lawrence stepped up the campaign, and in July he launched a daring raid on the key port of Aqaba, which fell to the Arabs on the 6th.

5 With flags flying, Lawrence's Arab troops make a triumphant entry into Aqaba, 6 July 1917. The second phase of the campaign now began, as the Arab guerrillas moved northward out of Arabia to operate on the desert flank of the British forces in Palestine. The British supplied their Arab ally with armaments, including armoured cars and light artillery, as well as gold to keep the tribesmen in the field now that they were far from their desert homes. The Arabs guarded the British forces' open (right) flank while attacking that of the Turks. The campaign came to a victorious military conclusion with Lawrence's and Feisal's entry into Damascus on 1 October 1918.

6 Feisal's bodyguard, camel-mounted tribesmen sworn to protect their leader.

From Gaza to Damascus
The war in Palestine

1 A German cavalry patrol in Palestine. As the quality of the Turkish Army in Palestine began to deteriorate, the hand-picked 'German Asia Corps' became increasingly more important.

2 A British 6in howitzer in action against the Turks near Gaza. The failings of British leadership in Palestine during the first two battles of Gaza (March and April 1917) led to the replacement of the British Commander-in-Chief, Sir Archibald Murray, by General Sir Edmund Allenby.

3 The Germans deployed a number of aircraft in Palestine and suitable counter-measures were adopted. Here Indian troops have set up a Lewis gun in order to provide anti-aircraft fire in the event of a German air-raid.

4 The official entry of the British into Jerusalem, 11 December 1917. To emphasise their Christian humility, Allenby and his staff walked through the gates to take possession of the city. Allenby had given Lloyd George his 'Christmas present to the British people', in what was otherwise a lamentable year for the Allied cause.

5 Turkish troops leap from their trenches to attack the British. Even after the defeat at the third battle of Gaza and the loss of Jerusalem, elements of the Turkish Army still fought well.

6 Turkish soldiers are searched by men of the 38th Lancashire Brigade after the engagement at Tuz Khurmath, 29 April 1918. Virtually abandoned by the Turkish High Command in Constantinople, the Turkish Army in Palestine began to disintegrate from the summer of 1918 onwards.

7 Indian lancers ride into Damascus, October 1918. The capture of Damascus marked the high-water mark of the Allied advance in Palestine, made possible by the crushing British victory at Megiddo, 19–24 September.

179

Campaign along the Tigris
British victory in Mesopotamia

1 The entry of British troops into Baghdad, 11 March 1917. The soldiers are part of a battalion of the Hampshire Regiment which had served continuously in Mesopotamia since early 1915. The British disaster at Kut (April 1916) led to the appointment of Sir Stanley Maude as Commander-in-Chief, Mesopotamia. An austere and devoted professional, Maude set about reorganising his command, which he had moulded into an effective fighting force when the offensive was resumed towards the end of 1916.

2 A river gunboat of the 'Insect'-class fires a broadside against Turkish positions by the Tigris. The shallow draught of vessels of this type (evident in the photograph) was useful, and their numbers rose steadily throughout 1917–18. Once Baghdad was in British hands, expeditions were mounted along the Euphrates and to the north of Baghdad to expel the Turks from southern Mesopotamia.

3 With bayonets fixed, British troops race forward to accept the surrender of a band of dispirited Turkish soldiers.

4 Armed with Lewis light machine guns, a detachment of the 7th North Staffordshire Regiment awaits action against Turkish troops holding the town of Kirkuk.

5 An 18-pounder in action against the Turks in Kirkuk, May 1918. British superiority in arms and equipment, combined with an overall numerical superiority, ensured that the far-flung Turkish garrisons had no hope of holding the British advance. After the collapse of Russia, Turkey looked to gain territory in the Caucasus and around the Caspian Sea – but was thwarted by the British.

6 Arab mounted police cross the dry bed of an old canal in Mesopotamia. Although far from enthusiastic about the idea, Maude was encouraged to make use of the anti-Turkish feelings of the Arab peoples and raise his own local Arab levies.

Baku and Persia

1 The oil derricks at Binagadi to the north of Baku, August 1918. The Caspian port of Baku was a major oil centre, and as the Bolshevik government in Moscow had no control over the southern areas of the old Russian Empire, a number of interested parties began to make plans to seize Baku. The main contenders were the White Russians, Turks, Germans and British, the latter concerned to prevent Baku falling into the hands of the Central Powers.

2 Under the command of Major-General Dunsterville, a British column – known as Dunsterforce – was dispatched from Baghdad to secure Baku. Here, men of the 7th North Staffordshire Regiment advance under Turkish machine-gun fire to capture oil wells around Baku.

3 Once in Baku the British tried to organise the local forces – White Russians and Armenians – against the Turks. Under British supervision, Armenian artillerymen fire a Russian-made 6in howitzer, August 1918.

4 A British Rolls Royce armoured car in action during the Dunsterforce expedition. The armoured car was based on a strengthened Silver Ghost chassis upon which was mounted a .303in Vickers machine gun.

5 Wearing full tropical gear British troops of Dunsterforce secure a railway culvert on the Baku–Digya road, August 1918.

6 Once Baghdad was under British control the oil wells in Persia were safe from Turkish attack. The Persians, however, resented the foreign domination of their country by Russia in the north and Britain in the south, and looked favourably towards the Central Powers. Here, a Russian armoured car patrols the streets of the capital, Teheran.

7 Poorly armed Persian soldiers are drawn up for inspection. Riven with destructive rivalries and lacking suitable military resources, Persia was forced into the role of bystander in the battle for Persian oil.

The Collapse of Bulgaria

1 Russian troops land at Salonika, July 1916. The idea of opening an offensive in the Balkans exercised a continuing fascination for the Allies, in spite of a multitude of political and military problems. The largest contingents of troops stationed in Salonika were from France and Serbia; alongside them were units from Italy, Britain and Russia. The Germans were amazed at this waste of manpower – 600,000 Allied troops in all were sent to Salonika – and sardonically described it as the 'greatest Allied internment camp' of the war.

2 The commander of a band of Greek Irregulars which fought with the British against the Bulgarians in Macedonia. The war divided the nominally neutral Greece into two factions, one pro-Allies, the other for the Central Powers. The Allied presence in and around Salonika was resented by many Greeks who saw it as an affront to national sovereignty.

3 Marching with their rifles 'at the trail', Italian troops of the 35th Infantry Division arrive at Salonika, 11 August 1916. Squabbles within the Allied command were a continuing block to military action.

4 Armed and uniformed by the French, expatriate Serbian troops fire a French 75mm field gun during the long-awaited Allied offensive against Bulgaria in September 1916. The hard-fighting Serbian Army wrested a strip of their territory back from the Central Powers, including the provincial capital of Monastir. Elsewhere, the offensive ground to a halt in the face of determined Bulgarian resistance.

5 A Bulgarian machine-gun detachment defends a position in the hills around Monastir. Supported by small units of Germans, the Bulgarian Army proved an effective force.

6 Gradually worn down by several years of war, by 1918 the Bulgarians feared that the Allies would deploy large tank forces against them. These dummy tanks were built to instruct Bulgarian infantry in anti-tank tactics.

7 The barrel of a British 2.75in mountain gun flies back at maximum recoil in a bombardment during the final offensive in Macedonia, September 1918. Under the dynamic leadership of General Franchet d'Esperey, the Allies at last broke through the Bulgarian lines; the Serbs regained their country, and the French (with British help) overran Bulgaria itself.

Vittorio Veneto
An Italian victory

1 Sited in a well-defended gun-pit, Italian artillerymen load a 6in gun. Following the stabilisation of the front line after Caporetto, there was little aggressive action from either side until June 1918, when the Austrians launched one last offensive. Poorly planned and quite beyond Austria's resources, it was easily repulsed, the net result for Austria being the loss of 150,000 men. While the armies of the Western Allies could rely on unlimited supplies – of food, equipment, munitions – the Austrian troops suffered badly, their uniforms in tatters, half-starved and racked by an epidemic of influenza.

2 Italian Marines scramble out from cover in support of the land forces during fighting in 1918.

3 Wearing gas masks, Italian troops guard a section of trench line on Podgora Hill. Fortunately for the Italians, the Austrians failed to use their gas shells effectively; during one attack in June a British unit was unaware that it had been under gas attack at all.

4 British artillerymen clean out a howitzer during a break in fighting on the Carso front. Three British divisions remained in Italy during 1918, along with contingents of French and American troops. The British 7th Division was to play an important part in the Italian victory at Vittorio Veneto in October, breaking through the Austrian lines on the right bank of the Piave.

5 Czech legionnaires within the Italian Army train with flamethrowers, prior to the final offensive against Austria in September 1918. Large numbers of Czechs had deserted from the Austrian armies and offered their services to any nation opposing the hated Hapsburg monarchy. Fighting for a national Czech state, the Czechs were regarded as more committed than the Italians.

6 Italian troops occupy the newly liberated town of Udine, part of the great exploitation that followed on from the Battle of Vittorio Veneto. The battle (from 24 to 30 October) completely destroyed the Austrian will to fight; for the Italians it was sweet revenge for Caporetto. The Austrians asked for an armistice which was signed on 3 November.

Armistice and revolution

1 At 11a.m. on 11 November 1918 World War I came to a close. For troops on the front line a sense of anti-climax prevailed, but in the towns and cities of the West massive celebrations began immediately. Here a French soldier is mobbed by a joyous crowd in Paris.

2 The scene outside Buckingham Palace on Armistice Day. Work stopped as news of the armistice came through and people thronged the streets to join in the celebration. Buses were commandeered and bonfires lit all over London in the evening. The celebrations lasted for three days, until the police were called in to restore public order.

3 Anglo-American *entente*: two convalescent British soldiers celebrate with a US sailor and an American Red Cross nurse, Paris, 11 November 1918. The wave of spontaneous joy that spread across Britain and France saw the temporary breakdown of social barriers as people expressed their relief that the killing was over.

4 Although Germany was forced to sue for peace because her armies had been beaten in the field on the Western Front, parallel to the collapse of the army was the breakdown of the old social order within Germany itself. Outright revolution was in the air in Berlin: in this photograph members of a newly appointed workers' and soldiers' council march up the Unter den Linden, 10 November 1918. The Kaiser had lost the support of the masses, and on 9 November he abdicated, leaving for exile in Holland, and a republic was declared at Weimar, under a new civilian government.

5 The new government had plenty of popular support but also many enemies, and left- and right-wing factions fought it out in the streets of Germany's towns and cities. Here far-left Spartacists occupy the offices of *Vorwärts*, a centre-left socialist newspaper.

6 News of the armistice is circulated to crowds gathering outside the Austrian Parliament, 11 November 1918.

Bibliography

C. Barnett, *The Swordbearers: Studies in Supreme Command in the First World War* (Penguin, 1963)

M. Brown, *Tommy Goes To War* (Dent, 1978)

G. Chapman, *Vain Glory* (Cassell, 1937)

A. Clark, *Aces High: The War in the Air over the Western Front 1914–18* (Fontana, 1974)

C.R.M.F. Cruttwell, *A History of the Great War 1914–18* (Granada, 1982)

Sir J. Edmonds, *A Short History of the First World War* (OUP, 1981)

C. Falls, *The First World War* (Longmans, 1960)

M. Ferro, *The Great War 1914–18* (Routledge & Kegan Paul, 1973)

P. Fussell, *The Great War and Modern Memory* (OUP, 1977)

R. Graves, *Goodbye To All That* (Penguin, 1981)

A. Horne, *The Price of Glory* (Penguin, 1964)

R. Hough, *The Great War at Sea* (OUP, 1983)

M. Middlebrook, *The First Day of the Somme* (Allen Lane, 1971)

D.B. Nash, *Imperial German Army Handbook 1914–18* (Ian Allan, 1980)

A. Norman, *The Great Air War* (Macmillan, 1968)

N. Stone, *The Eastern Front* (Hodder & Stoughton, 1975)

J. Terraine, *To Win a War: 1918 The Year of Victory* (Sidgwick & Jackson, 1978)

J. Terraine, *The Smoke and the Fire* (Sidgwick & Jackson, 1980)

J. Terraine, *White Heat: The New Warfare 1914–18* (Sidgwick & Jackson, 1982)

J. Terraine, *The First World War 1914–18* (Papermac, 1984)

Index